BLACK ISSUES IN SOCIAL WORK AND SOCIAL CARE

Mekada Graham

BASW

BRITISH ASSOCIATION
OF SOCIAL WORKERS

First published in Great Britain in 2007 by

The Policy Press
University of Bristol
Fourth Floor
Beacon House
Queen's Road
Bristol BS8 1QU
UK

Tel +44 (0)117 331 4054
Fax +44 (0)117 331 4093
e-mail tpp-info@bristol.ac.uk
www.policypress.org.uk

British Library Cataloguing in Publication Data
A catalogue record for this book is available from the British Library.

Library of Congress Cataloging-in-Publication Data
A catalog record for this book has been requested.

ISBN 978 1 86134 845 6 paperback
ISBN 978 1 86134 846 3 hardcover

Cover design by Qube Design Associates, Bristol.
Printed and bound in Great Britain by MPG Books, Bodmin.

In memory of Emilio Guyagen with love.

This book is also dedicated to Gloria Adassa Barnes,
a colleague and sister friend.

Contents

Acknowledgements

In writing this book, I am grateful for the support and assistance of many people, including my relatives and friends. First of all, my students both in Britain and in California and recently Oklahoma in the US, where my teaching in research, social welfare policy, cultural diversity and oppression have stimulated dialogue and discussion about social theory and social work and particularly black perspectives in social work. Special thanks to Dr Gillian Berry, Dr Emily Bruce, Dr Candence Wynter, Gil Robinson, Dr Gloria Gordon and the Black Academics Conference Committee (UK) for their encouragement in the development of this work. I would also like to acknowledge the spirit of my father because sometimes when pieces of writing became demanding I thought of him and his positive view of life and this helped to sustain me to move forward and to complete this work.

During completion of the final chapters of this book, my editor, Jo Campling, sadly passed away. I owe a debt of gratitude to Jo for her encouragement and enthusiastic support in writing this book. Jo approached me to undertake this project because she felt there was a pressing need for a social work text on black issues in social work and social care. I hope this book has helped to fill this gap in current literature. I would also like to thank my colleagues at California State University and the University of Oklahoma with extended thanks to Dr Richard Salsgiver and Dr Andrew Cherry for their helpful comments on several portions of the text.

Foreword

by Professor Ira Colby, University of Houston

Social work is a remarkable profession. Remarkable with regards to: its commitment to the education for competent, ethical practice; its range of both practice modalities and settings; the breadth of diversity of clients; and its application throughout the world. But what is most remarkable is the sheer audacity of the profession's mission – to realise justice for all people. Cynics, others might say 'realists', may well characterise social workers as idealistic individuals who are on an unattainable Don Quixote quest. The idea of achieving justice for some people, never mind all people throughout the world, is by itself a Herculean task and mind-boggling in view of its political, social and economic dimensions. For example consider the following.

At this moment in time the world's population is projected to be 6.5 billion (www.census.gov/ipc/www/popclockworld.html) in an estimated 228 countries (www.census.gov/ipc/www/idbr200608.html) and, according to the *Encyclopedia of Language and Linguistics* (Brown, 2006), there are more than 33,000 languages spoken around the world. The number of new countries, each with their own defining characteristics, beliefs and traditions, has changed and grown and will continue to change and grow in the future. Between 1900 and 1950, approximately 1.2 countries were created each year; from 1950 to 1990, 2.2 countries were organised each year; and in the 1990s, the number of new countries organised jumped to 3.1 countries annually (Enriquez, 2005).

No one can expect to gain even a rudimentary knowledge of the many countries of the world each with its own language and culture. Nor can we foresee which cultures and languages will be important or exist in the middle of the 21st century. Similarly, no one can predict with steadfast assurance and accuracy future events in local, national or international arenas.

The convergence of key, unrelated global social, political, economic and technological events that began in the 1980s and continue in the new century requires a different way of thinking and working with people around the world. *New York Times* writer Thomas L. Friedman (2005) argues that a new world order emerged at the outset of the 21st century that 'flattened' the world and, as a result, powerfully reshaped the lives of people in all quarters of the world.

Suffice to say, today we live in a different, more open world with fewer borders that separate or minimise our interactions. No matter who we are or where we live, all people are touched by distant wars, terrorist threats, hurricanes, typhoons, tsunamis, Middle East oil shortages, narcotics trafficking, irreversible destruction of our environment coupled with the threats caused by global warming, widespread, pervasive poverty, new and deadly diseases, trade wars and the daily threat posed by the growing world arsenal of nuclear weapons. All these events draw governments into new collaborative intergovernmental relationships.

These worldwide issues suggest that social workers today need to know more than earlier generations about international affairs and about other countries and cultures. Today's social worker should possess more than a passing interest in world news but clearly recognise that clients, be they individuals, families, groups, or communities, must be viewed through particular, unique racial, ethnic and/or cultural lenses. For a moment, consider these brief case scenarios.

Case 1

The client, age five, was referred to the Department of Child and Protective Services by a pre-school teacher, who observed the youngster being lethargic, a loner during group activities, and always wearing old, unkempt clothes. One day the class was asked to draw a picture of their homes; this child's depiction included a number of small stick figures – all with no hands and only small circles for a face with no mouth, nose, eyes or ears; the home had no windows; the yard included a number of trees, all with no leaves; and the background was coloured with black crayon. The referral noted that the child's sack lunch typically included one piece of buttered bread with sugar sprinkled on it and a piece of candy or fruit. The teacher was concerned and decided to make a home visit one afternoon where she found the child and three older siblings, aged seven, eight and nine, left at home alone.

Case 2

A mother called the NGO asking for help with her family, which she described as "falling apart". She and her husband had tried a variety of techniques they read about in the newspapers and learned about on TV shows, for example, 'time out rooms' and suspension of privileges, but to no avail. The older 14-year-old daughter sneaks out of the apartment at night and is dating a man in his mid-20s. The younger son, age nine, is becoming more withdrawn from the family and friends. For example, he no longer plays football with his friends in the afternoon but stays in his room. Dad is getting angrier, is on a 'short fuse', and is threatening to 'send' the daughter away to other relatives.

Certainly more information is warranted for a social worker to assess and create an effective intervention in either case. To what extent is it necessary to know the race and ethnicity of the clients? Does race and ethnicity add an important dimension to social work practice? How would our thinking change if we learned that the families were black? What if we learned that the child was African Caribbean or that her mother and father were from Kenya? Would it matter what region of the world she came from? To what extent does race and culture in these two examples add a dimension that forces the social worker to consider the influence of larger, macro-matters in the day-to-day lives of the child and the community? Or, should the social worker exempt the influence of race and culture in these two cases and focus solely on the presenting problem?

Since World War II and the passage of the 1948 British Nationality Act, the ethnic, racial and cultural character of the UK dramatically changed as the nation embraced multiculturalism as a dominant ideology. The social work profession in the UK also adopted this national ideology by embracing multiculturalism as a practice principle with its inclusion in the British Association of Social Workers Code of Ethics (British Association of Social Workers, 2003). And through policy – for example, the 1989 Children Act notes that culture is an important consideration for practice and the more recent 2002 Race Relations Act requires local authorities to provide apt services – a concerted effort is made to recognise the importance of race in practice.

In recent years a shift in thinking has begun, evidenced by significant government officials who have criticised multiculturalism. The British Government's Communities Secretary, Ruth Kelly, publicly warned that the promotion of cultural and religious difference would come at the expense of "national cohesion" in Britain (Tweedie, 2006). Building on Kelly's comments, Prime Minister Tony Blair, noted that "No culture or religion supersedes our duty to be part of the UK" (Johnson, 2006).

Critics of multiculturalism are not isolated in the UK nor limited to political arenas. More than 60 years ago, Swedish economist Gunnar Mydral (1944) noted the growing tension in the US between the promotion of a liberal human rights agenda and the nation's inability to realise this in black America. For Mydral, the solution was to rectify the prejudices embraced by whites or to improve opportunities for blacks. The pervasiveness of hatred towards blacks was evident, as he wrote, "… there is no doubt that the overwhelming majority of white Americans desire that there be as few Negroes as possible in America. If the Negroes could be eliminated from America or greatly decreased in numbers, this would meet the whites' approval" (p 167).

Throughout the second half of the 20th century, the US government created numerous affirmative action policies and programmes with the collective objective to realise social, economic and political justice for racial and ethnic minorities. Even so, affirmative action as a policy that recognises the uniqueness of racial and ethnic disparities continues to be attacked as a limiting force that discriminates against others. Thernstrom and Thernstrom (1999) voiced a common refrain among critics of such programmes noting that racial preference threatens a country's progress. Thomas Sowell, a senior fellow with the US-based Hoover Institution and a harsh critic of affirmative action programmes and other racially and ethnically directed public policies, contends that all people benefit from others' advantages while equality of opportunity supports a 'no fault of their own' mentality (www.manhattan-institute. org). In other words, race should not be considered in public policy nor, by extension, in professional practice. A 'colour-blind' approach is fair and just for all people.

The social work profession rejects the notion that we can and should live in a 'colour-blind' society. Social workers celebrate the richness and importance that race and ethnicity bring to a client's life situation. On the one hand, race and ethnicity are a source of incredible strength and opportunity while conversely racism, prejudice and discrimination threaten people's ability to maximise their abilities to live free and productive lives. Central to the social work profession's commitment to justice is the recognition and acceptance that a client's social history influences their current behaviour. While we understand that it is impossible to rectify the past and change what has happened, social workers acknowledge the role that race plays in a client's life. To do otherwise will only reinforce the past and buttress current race-based obstacles.

This book serves as an important reminder of the force that race plays in clients' lives and, as such, as a central consideration in social work practice. Early on, Mekada Graham states, "it is no longer acceptable to treat everyone in the same way or to provide care to individuals based on a set of norms drawn from the majority society" (p 4). Throughout this work, Graham builds and pulls together a well-rounded, compelling rationale that race be accepted as a critical practice consideration. The benefits of multicultural practice are many but most of all provide the social worker the needed framework for effective, client-centred practice.

Graham is correct when writing, "By presenting voices of those who are relegated to the outer edges of society, this brings together available information about lived experiences and the ways in which their background contributes to different experiences" (p 24). The practice of social work mandates the consideration and integration of the client's full life experiences. To ignore or downplay any one aspect of a client's life will only result in a less than successful resolution. The title of Cornell West's thought-provoking book, *Race Matters* (1994), offers in the simplest words the most compelling consideration necessary for the provision of competent, ethical social work practice.

ONE

Introduction

Social justice is at the heart of social work's mission because practitioners often work with people from communities that experience discrimination and injustice on the basis of an individual's race, gender, class, age, disabilities, sexual orientation, religious or spiritual beliefs, culture or health. Although other helping professions contribute to the well-being of individuals and society, social work is unique in its adoption of social justice as a guide for practice. There has been a great deal of change in social work in recent years but nonetheless these broader aspects of the profession remain. Practitioners carry out their tasks in a variety of settings, engaging in decision making and problem solving drawing on different methods that form part of professional policy and practice. This body of professional knowledge rests on a range of social science perspectives including the development of welfare policy and practice through the 19th century to the present.

In writing about social policy, Williams (2000) views this field of study as an exciting subject because it sheds light on how a society organises and manages social welfare but above all tells us about society's social and economic priorities, its hierarchies, its inequalities, its cultural practices and its responses to social change. This examination of society to understand more about welfare policies has immediate relevance to social work because the profession is not only deeply influenced by policy issues but also greatly influenced by similar forces. 'Welfare' is about people's lives, their experiences, personal opinions and beliefs and, as such, value judgements and ideas inevitably inform social work policy and practice (Adams, 2002). This places social work firmly in the political arena and helps to explain the vulnerability of professional knowledge to critique both inside and outside the profession as well as the need to expand its repertoire in response to changing needs and priorities.

Recent changes in social work have moved the profession in various directions. For example, the introduction of a mixed economy of social care and new approaches to management have advanced the fragmentation of social work tasks. These changes have transformed the day-to-day practice of many social workers by curtailing professional autonomy and caring aspects of practice and instituting procedure following, paperwork and budgets. As the nature of social work practice is repositioned, commentators have made reference to a 'crisis of identity' in the profession and concerns about its future relevance (Banks, 2001). These changes are not confined to Britain but have been observed across other parts of the world where shifts in patterns of social welfare reflect a decreasing role of the state in responding to vulnerable and disadvantaged groups.

Following the social movements of the 1960s and the radical social work movement in the 1970s and 1980s, social work began to develop critical practice theories that challenged the self-image of social work as a caring profession and its exclusive focus on personal and social circumstances. These developments transformed social work with greater attention paid to social structures and power relations between groups in society as a means of promoting social change. Despite the differences in approaches, this progressive force in the profession developed a broad range of theories including anti-racist and multicultural social work, feminist social work, various strands of community work, Marxist social work and action forms of research (Healy, 2000).

Although social work was one of the earliest disciplines to take on board issues of discrimination, social work institutions have been slow to respond and make necessary changes in provision and delivery of services to meet the needs and aspirations of black communities in particular. Early perspectives claimed that because welfare services are based on universal principles, they tended to produce a one-size-fits-all colour-blind service, with little room for flexibility. In addition, questions of entitlement and sometimes a culture of indifference also acted as a barrier to accessing appropriate services. As the decline of class-based analysis of social divisions took hold, the impact of oppression and discrimination on the basis of race, gender and other social categories began to receive more attention.

During the 1980s immigration issues featured highly in public debates about discrimination and these discussions entered social work. Social workers were often working with the view that black people should assimilate into the British way of life and social policies reflected this understanding, as well as a universal colour-blind set of services that ignored the particular needs of people from diverse communities.

A series of studies during the 1970s up to the present have provided evidence of persistent discrimination against black people in employment, housing, health and other services. With the introduction of the 1968 and 1976 Race Relations Acts, legislation provided the framework for policy intervention. A set of strategies such as equal opportunities policies emerged and was adopted by the public and later private sectors to tackle racism and to change organisational bias. These initiatives were viewed as necessary to promote equality, to ensure better race relations and to decrease exclusion.

Alongside these developments, black professionals, activists and anti-racists raised issues of racism and called for change in both policy and practice. The Association for Black Social Workers and Allied Professions (ABSWAP) was particularly active in campaigning for the social rights of black children and for the need for new initiatives in black communities, starting with the recruitment of black foster carers and adopters. This undertaking led to ABSWAP presenting evidence to the House of Commons Select Committee in 1983, which played a major role in shaping legislative reforms leading to the 1989 Children Act. For the first time, this Act placed a statutory responsibility on local authorities to give due consideration to racial origin, ethnic background, religion and language in the provision and delivery of services. The introduction of these reforms is one of the successful black-led efforts to bring about real change in social work policy and practice.

Black students in social work were also active in demanding changes in social work education, particularly with regard to practice, and raised concerns about the way they were treated in social work programmes. In response to this, several initiatives were introduced into social work education, including Paper 30, which led to controversial debates about the nature and extent of institutional racism in British society. Issues of oppression and discrimination were introduced into social work programmes to help prepare students to work with diverse communities and to deal with racism in social work institutions and practices.

Even though anti-racist social work was heavily criticised by the media and in public and academic circles more generally, this perspective opened attention to other forms of discrimination, and contributed to anti-discriminatory practice becoming part of the fabric of social work education and practice (Macey and Moxon, 1996). To a lesser extent, multicultural perspectives have also contributed to social work knowledge with recognition that much of the writing about social work and its history is derived from western cultures. Social work tends to reflect social assumptions that give more value to the importance of the individual, linking this approach to concepts of individual rights. Many cultures throughout the world tend to emphasise more community or family-oriented approaches based on social assumptions that are often linked to religious beliefs, social philosophies or worldviews. In recent years different forms of practice have developed in response to the inadequacies of western models of social work, which in turn have helped to modify conventional social work models.

While multicultural perspectives are widely accepted in the context of the US model of social work, many social work authors in Britain were sceptical of this approach because it was regarded as superficial and looked at cultural differences while ignoring issues of power and social justice (Dominelli, 1988). However, multicultural perspectives apply to a wide range of approaches including a critical approach to forms of oppression. As multicultural and anti-racist perspectives developed further, they tended to be separated by authors, so divisions emerged as issues of racism, individual and institutional, characterised anti-racist social work, whereas multicultural social work, however, dealt with issues of cultural difference, cultural sensitivity and competence. Anti-racist social work continued to be both promoted and maligned, with heated debates about the term 'race' and the nature and extent of racial discrimination in British society. Nonetheless, anti-racist social work opened up developments towards progressive practice and a working knowledge of the relationships between forms of oppression such as race and gender.

Multicultural approaches in social work and helping professions have become more popular in recent years with the introduction of cultural competence and sensitivity. Authors have introduced models and tools to enhance assessment skills and to remove communication barriers because it is no longer acceptable to treat everyone in the same way or to provide care to individuals based on a set of norms drawn from the majority society. The growth of social work as a profession throughout the world as well as the increasing diversity of national populations has drawn attention to the neglect of the life stories, histories and intellectual agendas emerging from black communities that are often not given serious consideration.

With regard to recent social policy, the Stephen Lawrence Inquiry (Macpherson, 1999) led to a sea-change in the public sector and substantiated the views of many people that racism permeates the structures and institutions of British society. Together with the passing of the 2000 Race Relations (Amendment) Act and acknowledgement that equal opportunities policies have not lived up to expectations in terms of addressing discrimination, new approaches were introduced replacing equal opportunities with a diversity framework, the new language of equal opportunities. The new Race Relations Act marks a social policy change towards valuing and promoting the positive aspects of diversity rather than an emphasis on avoiding discrimination.

Equally important, this legislation requires local authorities to promote equality and good relations between groups.

Aims and rationale of the book

Writing a book about black perspectives in the present climate is an ambitious task, beset with many dangers not least because of the many criticisms levelled at the very idea of black perspectives in social work. Some of these critiques are concerned with the difficulties in clearly defining the boundaries and content of black perspectives. Indeed, in writing this book, the author was aware of the difficulties in attempting to bring together the countless views from many different communities about issues in social work. However, the author decided to move ahead because of the belief that there is an overriding need for social work texts that bring some fresh thinking to bear on social work issues from different vantage points. As many authors have confirmed, one pattern of oppression in the wider society is an omission that works to exclude the ideas of black intellectuals and disregard the worldviews, interpretations, experiences and sociocultural perspectives of black communities (Young, 1990; Schiele, 2000; Graham, 2004).

In the British context, social work has been largely indifferent to the histories of social welfare of black communities and in some contexts suppressed their ideas, interests, cultural knowledge and experiences. With the inclusion of gender, race, ethnicity, disability and sexual orientations, social work still appears to have failed to adequately address the under-representation of black people as researchers and scholars. Indeed until very recently, there were no black female social work professors in Britain.

The general aim of this book is to encourage social workers, students and other professionals to develop a wider appreciation of the concerns and issues surrounding social work among black communities in Britain. For new students coming into social work, the principles of anti-discriminatory practice are given high priority as key building blocks for good practice. These approaches require tools to engage in thinking about the particular and the complexity of black people's experiences and to connect this to the realities of practice. Although progress has been made in some areas of social work practice, there still remains a pressing need for a more inclusive approach to understanding human growth and development. While there are no easy solutions to the ills confronting black communities in Britain, this book seeks to ask new questions in search of social understanding and human betterment.

When Ahmad published the successful text entitled *Black perspectives in social work* in 1990, social work issues from the vantage point of black communities were almost non-existent. Many social work students and practitioners had little choice but to refer to literature developed in the US, and although this material provided useful insights, it lacked a context of colonial histories, migration and the particular way social relations are organised in British society. One of the strengths of Ahmad's text is that it looked at critical issues in social work and articulated viewpoints based on collective struggles against racism, introducing new agendas that needed to be addressed.

As black perspectives began to develop into a body of writing, mounting critiques about the meanings of the terms 'race' and 'racism' seemed to break down the idea of a generalised understanding of racism and raise doubts about the viability of black perspectives. In addition, limitations in the use of the term 'black' to describe some visible minority groups began to surface as divisions in self-definition among black individuals and communities became more apparent. In these changing conditions there are different ways of being 'black' that are linked to social realities and experiences, and it is therefore important to avoid privileging one view over another.

However, in the midst of these challenges and concerns, a broader vision is taken that speaks to the possibilities of this project and looks to the contributions of Black Studies that have transformed academic life and the social sciences in many ways. Even though these developments have largely taken place in the US, they have nurtured a body of academic literature spanning various schools of thought and interests. At the outset, Black Studies engaged in necessary critiques of traditional disciplines in the social sciences and challenged the limitations, distortions and biases in conventional research methodology.

Following these developments, Black Studies opened up new avenues of human experience using a range of research methods. Although there are ongoing debates about the term 'Black Studies', its scope and attempts to redefine its boundaries, this interdisciplinary field of study has had a significant impact in articulating the hidden histories and cultural and intellectual agendas emerging from black experiences. These extensive contributions have brought Black Studies into higher education and attended to the virtual absence of black histories, lived experiences and understandings in the social world.

Using the development of Black Studies as a frame of reference, the author believes that black perspectives are still relevant and can generate much needed research agendas and literature to give opportunities for black researchers to make important contributions to social work theory and practice. There is no single model of black perspectives that can deal with the many diverse cultures and viewpoints within black communities but this is no reason to disregard the possibility of a body of work that can assist in many ways in dealing with the pressing needs of black communities in Britain.

There is currently already a growing body of literature by black academics in social work and this book contributes to these new and exciting developments. For too long the viewpoints and concerns of black individuals and communities and their experiences have been marginalised or neglected. By encouraging black perspectives as an overarching approach to social work, spaces can be opened up to allow voices to speak and grapple with central questions facing black individuals and communities. Another important issue is social agency and the need for critical voices to question existing academic knowledge underpinning the social constructions of black people.

Goldstein (2002) outlines the scope and character of black perspectives:

- Valuing black people (individually and collectively) and their right to self-define.
- Recognising black people's right to determine their own agendas.
- Recognising the strengths, commonality and diversity of black people.
- Struggling against racism in its daily manifestations.
- Valuing the multiple ways of constructing and understanding the world that black people have developed.
- [Valuing the contributions of black people to world history].

One of the features of black perspectives identified by Goldstein is that this approach treads a difficult line between valuing the individual and the collective and recognising that anti-racism is not the only defining parameter of black people. This way of looking at black perspectives helps to incorporate the complexities of modern life and identities.

Terminology

Having discussed the difficulties as well as the possibilities of black perspectives, the terminology used in this book is turned to. Again, there are many difficulties in using terms that will be acceptable to everyone. When talking about 'black communities' or 'black individuals' who do we actually mean? In this text the author will be talking about people of African Caribbean, African and Asian origin who reside in Britain as people of the postcolonial diaspora who share an experience of shared marginalisation and shared experiences of being the 'other' in Britain (Mizra, 1997; Rigg and Trehan, 1999).

In using this term the author recognises the limitations and the criticisms that are invited as some postcolonial people do not define themselves as 'black'. However, alternative widely accepted language such as 'black and ethnic minorities' or 'minority ethnic communities' suffer from similar difficulties and can be cumbersome throughout the text. The author is also aware that 'black and minority ethnic', abbreviated as BME, is in current usage in some literature; however, they are cautious about using this abbreviated form, as this is not a term the communities themselves tend to use. Suffice to say, the author is aware of the wide diversity among black communities and in no way assumes that there is universal agreement or that black communities are a homogeneous group. There is often a tension between the need to acknowledge differences yet at the same time to recognise some commonalities in terms of experiences and consequences of racism and structural inequalities.

Another related point is that the outlook and composition of black communities is undergoing many changes as new communities come to Britain. This enforced migration has taken place through wars and disasters that have left people traumatised as they are seeking a new life elsewhere. Bearing this in mind, there are particular life experiences or issues surrounding asylum-seekers and refugees that require more depth than is possible in this text. The author is also mindful of recent events that have exposed religious discrimination in many areas of social life that also require deeper inquiry and as such there are limitations in any text attempting to deal with a wide range of topics in social care and social work pertinent to black communities.

Social work

Social work is a profession concerned with people and their environment and seeks to intervene to assist in dealing with complex problems and difficulties people face in their lives. Professional social work is focused on assisting people to reach their full potential and engages in problem solving and social change. With changes in the welfare system and an increasing range of activities, social work occupies an ambiguous position as many activities traditionally undertaken by social workers are now carried out by other welfare professionals. In this text the term 'social worker' is used to refer to people who are paid to undertake professional tasks including social care activities.

Social care

As the need for social care has grown over the years, care services have been organised as separate activities distinguished from medical and nursing care. Social care describes a range of services available for adults in need. These social care services cover personal care and practical assistance, as well as opportunities for socialising and leisure activities. Social care also includes domestic tasks and relates to improving quality of life. As this text covers chapters on ageing and disability, social care is an important feature to these practice areas.

Children in public care

The term 'looked after children' was introduced by the government and the 1989 Children Act (England and Wales), and is the term used for children cared for by local authorities. In the past 'children in care' was the term in general usage and international audiences understood this term. In this text the term 'children in care' or 'children in public care' is used.

Clients and users

The term 'client' was in general usage in social work texts for people who use social work services. With changes in the way welfare services are delivered the term 'service user' has been widely adopted. However, the author has tended to stick to 'client' although in some areas has made reference to 'service user'. There are connotations associated with these terms and some of the issues concerning the use of these terms are discussed in the following chapters of the book.

Structure of the book

The first two chapters provide readers with an introduction to anti-discriminatory practice as well as an overview of oppression and social divisions. Against this background, major client groups are considered – children and families, people with mental health problems and older people.

Chapter Two gives a general overview of the historical development of anti-discriminatory practice. It begins by looking at how anti-racist social work emerged with discussions about the influence of sociology and race relations theories in shaping social work theory and practice with black families. As social work draws on the social sciences for its development of professional knowledge, as a base for human behaviour, sociology and psychology greatly influence and inform practice. Following on, there are brief sections that focus on anti-racist social work and power, colonial histories and finally issues of culture in social work.

The major theme of Chapter Three is to look at different forms of oppression in the light of postmodern perspectives and their relevance for social work. The chapter begins with an overview of models of oppression and seeks to unravel some of the complexities before moving on to anti-discriminatory practice, bringing together common themes. The influence and debates about postmodern perspectives and black perspectives are discussed with brief outlines of theories emerging from black feminist thought and African-centred theories of social change and cultural identities as well as issues of power. A brief overview of white privilege is also presented because there is a growing recognition that by exclusively focusing on issues of racism white privilege tends to be unrecognised or not even acknowledged. The chapter closes with an examination of diversity as the new language of equal opportunities and implications for social care.

Chapter Four is the longest chapter in the book because children and families has been one of the most controversial areas of practice in social work. The chapter starts with an overview of the background and context to working with black families and children and looks at key policy issues. After this, empowerment within the context of the 1989 Children Act is discussed, including reference to empowerment-oriented practice. The next section presents an overview of black children in public care, with an emphasis on key policy issues. The chapter then goes on to consider the difficulties facing black young people leaving care with reference to a new framework for leaving care services within the 2000 Children (Leaving Care) Act (England and Wales).

Child abuse and neglect are important areas of social work and this chapter highlights the lack of research about child maltreatment in black families, looking at how social work has responded. There is an overview of a 'social' perspective of childhood and its implications for social work practice with children. A social model of childhood has been applied to social work practice with black children because this model offers the opportunity for black children to voice their lived experiences within the context of societal racism that can offer not only recognition of their lives in the fullest sense, but also protection. Drawing on these themes, there is a discussion of the Victoria Climbié Inquiry and new initiatives within the 2004 Children Act – *Every Child Matters* (DfES, 2004)

Chapter Five takes a critical look at mental health and social work. For many years there has been a high presence of black people in mental health services and the first section of this chapter explores social policy developments such as the 1983 Mental Health Act and community care, and more recently the *National Service Framework for mental health* (DH, 1999). The chapter moves on to look at issues of racism in mental health services and the growth of mental health users' movements and their participation in the provision and delivery of services. As black people with mental health problems feel marginalised in many service user groups, there is a discussion of empowering mental health users by applying a recovery model that builds on strengths and offers hope along the road to recovery. The next section of the chapter charts the development of black psychology as well as taking a brief look at alternative and holistic approaches to mental health and well-being. The final section offers a brief discussion about spirituality and social work.

The disability movement has brought about changes in the way disability is defined and has criticised models of social work that seemed to encourage dependency and a passive outlook. As these developments unfolded, Chapter Six reviews these changes and the successful challenges to the medical model of disability. After a brief history of social policy towards disabled people, the moral, medical and social model of disability are outlined. The social model of disability is examined and applied to black disabled people. Further, there is a discussion of the double jeopardy or double discrimination model, and its inadequacy in understanding the social realities of being black and disabled is pointed out. A social model of disability underpins the introduction of strategies that support independent living. Recently, direct payment schemes have been introduced to assist in this effort but several issues have arisen surrounding this individualised approach and this section grapples with these questions.

Chapter Seven considers ageing, and begins by looking at current issues in social policy and ageing with an emphasis on older black people. Social policies and their impact on older people are reviewed. The recent introduction of the *National Service Framework for older people* (DH, 2001b) and research findings from the Race Equality Unit are also discussed. In addition, older black women and their vulnerability to poverty and health issues are considered. As groups of older black people become more visible, issues of migration begin to surface and this section looks at the challenges for both older people and their families. The chapter then moves on to explore models of ageing including ageing and the life course, successful ageing and ageing in different cultures. The final section of this chapter looks at life histories and social work and their importance in documenting the lived experiences and oral histories of black communities.

The final chapter returns to the main themes of the book. As social work responded to issues of discrimination, racism and social inequalities, anti-discriminatory practice and cultural issues entered social work education and professional practice. These important areas underpin critical practice with a range of client groups. Social policy plays an important role in shaping social work interventions as well as developing services and allocating resources. Universal approaches to social welfare underpin the welfare state and continue to be the established framework for social policy development. However, this approach to policy formulation appears to overlook the specific circumstances of some black communities. After discussions about social policy, the issues pertaining to each client group are summarised, together with policy implications and future possibilities.

TWO

Anti-discriminatory social work in context

Introduction

In the past, issues of discrimination and oppression were not considered particularly important in social work theory and practice. Conventional models of social work largely ignored the social experiences of many groups and common forms of practice reflected biases found in the historical periods from which they emerged. Early perspectives in social work were more concerned with inequalities in relation to social class and little attention was paid to the social divisions of race and gender. Even though many social workers were aware of the economic and social disadvantages experienced by black people, the issues of racism and discrimination were largely overlooked in social policies and the profession over time has struggled to change its practices to better serve individuals and communities.

However, since the 1980s there has been a growing body of literature that seeks to address many forms of discrimination and inequalities through integrating theories and practice principles into social work and social care (Dominelli, 1988, 2002; Thompson, 1993, 2003; Dalrymple and Burke, 1995; Adams et al, 2002a). Anti-racist social work provided the starting point for these critical approaches towards practice. Anti-racist social work practice was adopted by social work education in the 1980s in what is known as Paper 30 (CCETSW, 1989).

After the introduction of anti-racist frameworks into social work training, this approach came under intense scrutiny. Concerns were expressed about the term 'race', its meanings and the extent to which racial discrimination was embedded in British institutions as well as society more generally. Some social work educators were uneasy about the theories underpinning anti-racist social work that appeared to be "informed by neither sociological, political nor economic theory or research" (Macey and Moxon, 1996, p 297). These discussions attracted wide media attention that branded these initiatives as promoting 'political correctness'. These critiques were also fuelled by the approach taken in many race awareness training (RAT) courses that focused on racism as a personal problem of white individuals.

Following these criticisms, the Central Council for Education and Training in Social Work (CCETSW) subsequently revised its rules and requirements towards anti-discriminatory practice for the Diploma in Social Work (CCETSW, 1991, 1995). This approach to practice included wider forms of discrimination such as gender, disability and ageing. More recently, anti-oppressive practice with its emphasis on power and structural inequalities has evolved to encompass a range of critical theories. At the same time, the term 'diversity' is increasingly being used in many social contexts to promote equality. This term is derived from human resource literature in the US and describes census-based categories across a range of social groups. These categories include race, ethnicity, gender, disability and age emerging from the historical experience of widespread immigration. In the UK context, diversity seeks to take account of an individual's multiple identities, which may include varied forms of discrimination. For example, an older black woman may experience discrimination because of age, race and/or gender.

This chapter considers anti-racist social work because it not only made a significant contribution to the profession in its own right but also paved the way for other forms of oppression to enter social work frames of reference. Anti-racist social work is explored within the context of underpinning knowledge primarily from sociological theories about race relations. Following on from this, black perspectives are considered because they have tended to be marginalised or excluded in many social work texts. Anti-racist social work offers a space for these approaches to be articulated. This chapter also explores anti-racist social work in practice and briefly considers issues of culture in social work.

Background and development of anti-racist social work

In contrast to other helping professions, social work is unique in its concerns about what is just and unjust in responding to human needs. These features of social work have given meaning to its mission and professional legitimacy (Reamer, 1993). Bearing this in mind, the profession has been able to develop its own response to discrimination in different ways, seeking social reform in favour of oppressed groups. Social change also plays a key role in social work's commitment to social justice and human well-being. In this regard, social work has a history of activism and critical traditions that seek to diminish systems of oppression and privilege on behalf of populations at risk (Stepney, 2005).

In seeking to activate social change, critical perspectives have developed through various social theories outside the profession to form a body of progressive practice theories. This broad range of theories includes anti-racist and multicultural social work, anti-oppressive and anti-discriminatory social work, feminist social work, radical social work and community work. The social movements of the 1960s provide the backdrop for these developments, when feminist and black struggles for equality raised questions about long-standing political, social and economic oppression. For example, black scholars and community groups in the US came together to address the marginalisation of black people to the fringes of society, and sought to bring their intellectual traditions, histories, social experiences, narratives and cultural ideas into academic study.

Black Studies emerged out of black struggles for equality, and developed into an area of study about African Americans but more recently has expanded to include those of African descent throughout the diaspora. Black Studies engaged with traditional disciplines in the social sciences and mounted a powerful critique of 'race' theories and paradigms that informed and justified racial inequality. In this instance, black sociologists uncovered biases in research studies in relation to black families and set about rewriting their histories and social realities and understandings from a black perspective (Billingsley, 1968; Hill, 1971; Nobles, 1978). These developments emerging from black experiences, histories and cultures opened up new research agendas where a community's own interpretation of social life was uncovered. In this way, a more inclusive picture became apparent, providing invaluable sources of material across the spectrum of human experiences.

In the UK, many black communities sought inspiration and ideas from the civil rights movements and black politics that exerted considerable influence in developing strategies of resistance to the historical burdens of racism in British society. Against this background, a handful of black researchers began to challenge the Eurocentric bias and issues of racism in the theoretical and practice framework of social work (Small, 1984; Ahmad, 1989, 1990; Maximé, 1993; Ahmad and Atkins, 1996). Through these activities, black perspectives came about as a critical form of practice. However, the British social work community has been somewhat reluctant to accept the credibility of black perspectives or to fully realise their potential for understanding the wider social context and lived experiences of black communities. As Ahmad (1989, p 155) points out:

> ... if present and future researchers and workers are to accept and realize the valuable contribution of a black perspective they will need to acknowledge that to disregard the emergence of a black perspective in Britain is tantamount to disregarding the American black experience as well, mainly because it is often argued that there are more similarities than differences between black American and black British experience. For this reason the black perspective in Britain has continuously referred to the knowledge base of black American research and made necessary adaptations to fit in with British experience.

From these beginnings, the profession has seen a growing body of literature that articulates an array of black British perspectives in social work and social care (Ahmad, 1990; Barn, 1993; Robinson, 1995; Banks, 1999a; Bernard, 2001; Bhuik, 2002; Graham, 2002, 2006a, 2006b). Over time social work has become more attuned to the impact of structural forces and operations of power on people's lives as an important component of practice interventions. For example, both empowerment- and strengths-based practice draw on listening to, respecting and responding to the voices and aspirations of service users. These practice developments emphasise lived experiences and the sociocultural aspects of people's lives as critical to understanding situations and in creating intervention strategies to meet their needs. These shifts in social work perspectives point out the value of giving voice to the lived experiences of oppression in various contexts and situations.

Sociology and race relations theories

Sociology plays an important role in providing professional knowledge for social work. Much of this literature draws on sociological ideas and the development of theories to explain and understand the processes that produce social divisions. Social class tended to be the main social division and focus of study that underpinned knowledge in social work. Poverty, deprivation, homelessness, poor health and lack of education and other social problems were explained in terms of long-standing class divisions. These concerns referred to the need for economic and social reforms as well as attention to failing social welfare institutions.

This model of deprivation and poverty failed to acknowledge other structural forces such as racism, sexism and discrimination, as well as the specific needs of black people and women. It was widely believed that racism was an attitude or personal prejudice that would weaken over time as the majority society accepted black communities. These individualised understandings of racism and discrimination framed much of the discussions in the 1960s and 1970s (Rose, 1969).

The emergence of new social movements, such as feminist and black civil rights movements, hastened the decline of class as the sole model of inequality in society. The model of social class seemed inadequate to account for a range of social divisions in society, and increasingly race and gender and other oppressions required study in their own right. These factors led to the growing interest in the study of race relations and the ways in which racial and ethnic divisions shaped interactions between minority and majority communities.

Assimilation

Drawing on the North American experience, sociologists in Britain began to adopt theories of assimilation to describe the process of adjustment of black 'immigrants'. This framework became the centre of interest in understanding the social relations between black people and the host society. These ideas were expressed in the term 'melting pot', which assumed black and minority ethnic communities would adopt the norms and values of the wider society and become 'British' in their outlook and thinking. This was to be achieved by integrating models of assimilation into social policies and ensuring that the implementation of these strategies caused minimal disruption to the society at large.

For example, in some local authorities some educational policies were designed to disperse immigrant children to less 'concentrated' areas (Tomlinson, 1977). According to Gillborn (2001), these practical measures were implemented to protect the stability of the educational system and to calm the fears of parents so that the progress of their own children would not be undermined by the undue preoccupation of teaching staff with the linguistic and other difficulties of immigrant children. These issues were discussed within a political climate of intense hostility towards immigration in the mass media and society generally. As a result of these debates in political and public circles, immigration became increasingly racialised. This close association between race and immigration has continued to surface over time through to contemporary policy debates in the media and elsewhere.

In this instance, 'asylum-seekers' has become the new code word for largely hostile responses to black people and immigration.

Social work was also influenced by ideas of assimilation and most social workers believed that this was the best approach to incorporate into practice (Barn, 1993). By accepting assimilation as the main goal in practice and service delivery, the cultural values and understandings of black communities were perceived as deficits or problematic and, therefore, should be discarded in their adopted society. Dominelli (1988) argues that the social worker–client relationship does not operate in a vacuum and that practitioners are influenced by popular beliefs in the wider society. Indeed, sets of ideas and values in professional practice are largely a reflection of majority, mostly middle-class, thinking. These concerns prompted several authors to question social work's image as a caring profession that advocates for populations at risk because black clients' needs were often ignored or they were subject to individual or institutional racist practices (Williams, 1987; Dominelli, 1988).

As black people were often portrayed as 'immigrants' in the wider society, they were viewed as having little or no entitlement to social welfare even though black communities have been an integral part of British society spanning several generations. These widespread beliefs were sometimes used to justify differential treatment towards black people as an 'undeserving' group (Fryer, 1984; Graham, 2002). With this course in mind, black people were expected to fit into services already provided and a 'like it or lump it' attitude prevailed across social services (Cheetham, 1982). It was felt that there was no need to consider the specific needs and concerns of black communities as the universal nature of social services would provide an adequate service for all. In fact, this colour-blind approach was felt to be appropriate to avoid 'a white backlash' against any 'special' provisions for black and minority communities. The overall effect of these practices was to exclude or marginalise black families. By focusing on psychodynamic approaches, many practitioners neglected critical social and political perspectives in explaining individual or family difficulties. As a result, these methods were implemented to assist in the assimilation of black people into the majority society.

As Bryan et al (1985, p 112) point out, some black families were deemed unsuitable for social work intervention:

> … whether we are single parents, homeless young women or the parents of children in care, we are constantly confronted with racist, classist or culturally biased judgments about our lives.

As theories of assimilation resulted in deficit models of black and minority families, it was assumed that western norms, values and culture were superior and problems experienced by black families were due to their failure to adapt to their new life and British society. As a consequence of these negative viewpoints, black families were lumped together and labelled as a 'problem' in the broader society. Black families were perceived as contributing to their own problems due to their cultural patterns or practices. The adoption of assimilation as a framework for practice also encouraged a colour-blind approach in childcare practice. Ahmad (1989) outlines the rationale of this approach in working with black children and their families:

1. Integrating black children into mainstream British culture helped to develop harmonious race relations.
2. Integration was in the interests of black children as they would accept western culture and forgo the maintenance of a separate identity.
3. Making changes in childcare services for black children would work against assimilation and would therefore be discriminatory.

Deficit models

During the 1970s, sociology produced research and literature concerned with social problems and deviancy, such as the rising divorce rate, single parents, homelessness and crime. Race relations and the 'problems' of immigration and black families were drafted into this field of study, which reinforced negative views already prevalent in society (Worsley, 1973). Solomos and Bulmer (2004) maintain that the negative representation of black people in many sociological texts was due in part to resources made available to study racial and ethnic minorities only as 'social problems' and as culturally deprived. The cultures and worldviews of black communities were ignored or relegated to the margins of research agendas. Lawrence (1982) is critical of sociology for its racist thinking that came together with models of assimilation to present black families as 'problematic' or dysfunctional. These viewpoints were translated into different ideas about African Caribbean and Asian families.

First, African Caribbean families were often perceived as disorganised and characterised as having weak family ties. According to this perspective, these characteristics of black families were caused by historical experiences of enslavement and economic hardship that had become an integral part of black families' structure and functioning.

By taking this approach, black families were seen as failing to take responsibility for their children and for supervision of young people.

Second, Asian families were perceived to have 'strong' cultural ties yet they caused 'problems' for British society because of their marked difference in culture, language and practices (Skellington and Morris, 1992). These ideas and concerns filtered into social work practice and professional judgements, helping to maintain the idea that 'problems' resided in black families who were having trouble adapting to life in Britain (Turney, 1996). Social work did not see itself as part of the problem in reproducing discrimination within the profession and in various ways was indifferent to racial discrimination and inequality that impacted on the lives of black people. As Penketh (2000, p 53) notes:

> ... black people's behaviour and family life were evidently judged particularly harshly by social work professionals, especially in terms of mental health and childcare, revealing that black parents are more likely to have their children removed and placed in residential and foster care.

Several research studies continued to document the adverse social conditions experienced by black and minority communities. Widespread discrimination was found in the labour market, housing, education and health services and, as a result of these factors, black and minority communities experienced high unemployment or the lowest position in the job market as well as the worst housing conditions in inner-city areas (Brown, 1984). A series of anti-discrimination legislation was introduced from the 1960s to 1970s in attempts to mediate the effects of discrimination (Race Relations Acts, 1965, 1968, 1976). These Acts sought to make it unlawful to discriminate against black and minority communities and to eradicate openly discriminatory advertisements. However, as Brown (1992) maintains, the initial impact of the Acts was encouraging, but progress towards equality of outcomes has been painfully slow. Distinct gaps between majority and minority employment patterns have emerged showing unemployment as a major source of inequality among young black and minority communities. The Acts were followed by the introduction of equal opportunities policies in the 1980s as a strategy to combat and eliminate inequalities in attempts to be 'fair to everybody'.

Understanding racism

There are many definitions of racism and many authors have des
racism as an ideology or set of beliefs that proposes that certain grouբ
superior to other groups based on their physical appearance. In the past ⸍⸍ப
present, these ideas are powerful and have been associated with enslavement,
persecution, violence and hierarchy. They have been used to justify inequalities
and discrimination. Although the idea of differences between people has no
biological basis, these beliefs have social and political meaning and, therefore,
race is a historical, social and political construct.

As our understanding about racism has grown, it is widely accepted that this
kind of discrimination is complex and changes according to political and social
conditions. Fredman (2001, p 2) explains:

> There is no single racism, but multiple racisms; colour racism must be
> examined together with cultural racism, which includes ethnicity, religion
> and language.

This means that there is more than one explanation or theory of racism. It is
recognised that racism operates and is maintained through social relations that
set in motion cycles of disadvantage and discrimination. Racism continues to have
a profound effect on the lives of black people or members of minority groups
in key areas such as education, employment and housing.

Cultural racism

This form of racism has emerged in recent years and as the shift away from
discrimination based on physical appearance towards cultural differences. This
is apparent in the way cultures are perceived as problematic because they are
'different' from the norm. This is often referred to as a set of 'new racisms'. The
language of cultural racism conceives other cultures as being pathological and
causing problems for the dominant society.

Institutional racism

After the Stephen Lawrence Inquiry (Macpherson, 1999) institutional racism
became an important way of understanding racism in the cultures of organisations
and their social practices.

Van Soest and Garcia (2003, p 16) describe institutional racism as follows:

Institutional racism is hidden behind the standard practices of hard-working, well-meaning White people. Institutional racism typically is not ugly. Rather than being expressed through racial slurs, it tends to be wrapped in noble proclamations of tradition, fairness and high standards.

Anti-racist social work and power

At the heart of anti-racist social work are issues of power and privilege. This is because inequalities stem from the exercise of power at the individual and structural level. Dalrymple and Burke (1995, p 15) explain that "our understanding of power has been shaped by the values we hold and the ideas we have about the society we live in". The idea of power can best be understood as relational. This means it is apparent in social relationships that exist between individuals and social groups (Gil, 1994). Conventional social work has long been criticised for its emphasis on personal weaknesses and an individualised understanding of problems.

Taylor (2004) identifies the consequences of adopting this individualised approach in understanding social problems in social work. Here, public issues are reframed into private pathologies of individual families and children. The divisions between the individual and society have been the subject of long-standing debates in social work. However, the focus on individualism at the expense of structural explanations has particular consequences for black families because there is a general pattern of denying legitimacy to racialised analyses and protests in British society and many factors that push issues of race to the outer edges of majority interest or concern (Crozier, 2001). The consequences of black communities' marginal status is often hidden under the surface of universal and colour-blind approaches that remain embedded in research agendas as well as much of the underpinning knowledge for social work.

Key points: Anti-racist social work

- Understanding how racism, oppression and discrimination impact on access to services, and opportunities that are essential for creating a full and rewarding life.
- Awareness of personal bias, stereotypes, attitudes.
- Motivation to learn about the lived experiences of others whose lives are different from one's own and the strengths utilised by those individuals and groups.
- Advancing the view that social identity influences knowledge development and ways of knowing and the need to include those historically marginalised in the construction of knowledge.

Source: Adapted from Van Soest and Garcia (2003)

Black perspectives and approaches in social work

As social work addresses many different social and economic conditions in society, the profession has been influenced by shifts in social theory and intellectual thinking about arrangements in social life. Indeed, social work as a profession is embedded in social welfare policy charged with the responsibility to deal with the social ills of society. As anti-racist social work established new thinking about racism and oppression, this approach also embraced black perspectives as a political and social understanding of black experiences. Young (1989) believes one of the consequences of tackling racism is that it undermines the dominant groups who rely on the continued oppression of others to maintain their status.

The issues of voice, representation and power relations have had an important place in bringing recognition and presence to those excluded along the lines of race, gender and class. As social movements of the 1960s and 1970s gathered pace, marginalised groups set about addressing their virtual absence in mainstream texts. These new forms of knowledge explored social experiences and hidden histories from different vantage points and entered the social sciences, including social work. On behalf of black minorities and women, questions emerged about conventional knowledge in the social sciences showing its biases and interests of dominant groups. As these criticisms surfaced, it became clear that knowledge in the social sciences could no longer be considered neutral in observing social relations. Because social work draws on social science disciplines as its underpinning knowledge, new developments across the various fields of study helped to reshape the profession to make marginalised voices heard.

Black perspectives in social work opened up a forum for marginalised groups to voice their social experiences and intellectual agendas. In this way, a more inclusive picture of social welfare emerges that includes the histories, cultures and philosophies of marginalised groups as a source of knowledge in anti-racist social work practice. The opening up of black experiences has also revealed dimensions of oppression that operate in different ways. One of the ways this kind of oppression functions is to create processes that silence certain voices or groups in society. Issues of silencing have long been a subject of discussion among many black authors in trying to understand how these processes work. Gordon (2001, p 319) explains:

> … in coming into an understanding of my own silences I was to conceptualise silence as a social construct, critical to maintaining the societal taboo around race and racism in British society. The demand for silence around race was, I came to understand, tantamount to self-denial of my realities, including my 'Blackness'. In most cases this enforced silencing is further institutionalised within the system through the self-silencing born of frustration when it seems that the racial issue runs so deep and so wide as to make it unfathomable and a situation which, as Blacks, we must merely to accept our lot in life. Exploring my practice enabled me to see that silence is a group's safety net and how the alienation and invisibility that I experienced, particularly in groups where I was in the token solo role, were the natural outcome of this function.

Dominant groups tend to construct society as simply 'theirs' on the basis of social and economic privilege. This means dominant groups behave as though their voices are the important ones and know what is good for others so that black minorities tend to remain on the edges of society, only becoming visible through stereotypes and problems that are likely to affect or concern the majority (Young, 1990). For example, this invisibility is apparent in mainstream social work texts, in particular histories of social work that exclude any mention of social welfare in black communities. As a consequence of this process the intellectual agendas and welfare concerns among black communities tend to be ignored.

By presenting voices of those who are relegated to the outer edges of society, this brings together available information about lived experiences and the ways in which their background contributes to different experiences. In another context, the experiences of oppression tend to place one in a position to speak about those experiences in various ways that are sometimes not understood by the wider society. Graham and Robinson (2004, p 662) make the point that: "speaking about individual experiences of racism allows us to consciously engage in exploring our realities, sharing knowledge of lived experiences and ways to 'get through' in and of the world".

Colonial histories

Colonialism is an important aspect of black histories that has particular significance in understanding social relations in contemporary British society. From the Middle Ages until well into the 19th century European colonial powers invaded, occupied or claimed large areas of the world. The impact of colonialism changed the direction of world history. For the countries of Africa and Asia they were unable to develop, with interference that often distorted or destroyed many indigenous structures and institutions. In many African countries, the colonial era also included the enslavement of African people taken by force to the Americas and elsewhere. The history of colonialism is marked by conquest, occupation and the forced administration of peoples outside of Europe.

As European colonial power expanded, a sense of superiority both racial and cultural had taken hold so that people outside of Europe were locked into representations as primitive or uncivilised people. In the meantime, Europeans constructed themselves as rational, modern and scientific. Through the process of colonialism, cultural and racial distinctions between the Europeans and colonised populations were established. The European settlers constructed an 'expatriate' culture that reinforced the cultural gap between the colonised populations and their rulers. The ideas of racial and cultural superiority filtered into British popular culture and were reproduced through notions of empire and the greatness of Britain.

The British Empire became firmly embedded in popular consciousness and these images had particular consequences for black people who settled in Britain in the 1950s and 1960's. For example, celebrations and ceremonies on Empire Day were underscored by racial and cultural superiority in reproducing dominant stereotypes and images of black people. In understanding how these historical markers are relevant in British society today, Noble (2005) points to the way that Britain, despite its imperial history, has managed to hold on to a sense of itself as an innocent island nation. This is in part because British people were sealed off from the brutish realities of colonial rule and it was the postwar migration of people from the Commonwealth that brought British people finally into close proximity with their previous colonial subjects. Black communities in Britain are a constant reminder of Britain's colonial past and although black people have been subject to 'race' and racism as a defining marker of difference, this is another layer added to the firmly established class structure that bears traces of colonial caste systems.

Histories of social welfare in black communities

Even though black communities have been an integral part of British society spanning several generations, their social welfare histories have been largely ignored in social work texts. As a result of this process, important contributions to the well-being of black communities and the relief of human suffering have rarely been documented or discussed (Graham, 2002, 2004). Examples of social welfare histories tend to be closely tied to black activism and resistance to racism and oppression in British society.

One of the beginnings of black activism can be traced to the enslavement of African people, men, women and children in Britain, who were bought and sold as chattels or commodities (Fryer, 1984; Lorimer, 1992). The growing African community in London during the 1700s consisted of enslaved and some 'free' African people and, according to Banton (1972), towards the end of the 18th century, two per cent of the population were people of African descent. The majority of the enslaved African population consisted of children and young people, a pattern reflected within the enslaved population in the Americas and the Caribbean (Myers, 1993). The community also included people who had arrived after enlisting to fight for Britain during the American War of Independence, for which they were promised their freedom.

During the 18th and 19th centuries the social welfare needs of black people were regarded as satisfied through the institution of enslavement and therefore access to Poor Relief was largely denied. Myers (1993, p 53) confirms the precarious position of black people in that "they failed to be cushioned by the safety net of the poor relief and the law consistently ruled that blacks brought to England were not hired servants and therefore not entitled to wages". There are early examples of community responses to social need that were located in efforts to secure freedom from enslavement. Black communities in London established clubs to support those who were destitute and who had evaded capture.

It is difficult to imagine successful leadership given the extent of hardship and deep-seated racism present in 18th-century Britain, yet a group of black men calling themselves the 'Sons of Africa' emerged as a political and social organisation. This organisation set about planning ongoing resistance and the end of enslavement through mobilising black communities and concerned individuals. They supported community demands for wages for work and celebrated legal victories. These struggles for a better and fairer society developed concerns about the social welfare needs of black people and their families. In the early decades of the 20th century organisations such as the Pan-African Federation and the League of Coloured Peoples actively supported black rights, provided assistance for families in need and gave help in finding accommodation.

Debates and concerns: black perspectives

One of the major criticisms of black perspectives in social work has been its difficulty in defining the boundaries of its content. However, according to Ahmad (1990, p 3), black perspectives should not be confined by distinct boundaries or language forms because they are rooted in long-standing histories of oppression and subordination across several groups and communities:

> ... a black perspective has no neat and tidy definition, neither is it just a string of words. A black perspective is more than a statement against 'white norms', it is an expression of assertion that cannot be bound by a semantic definition. The factors that prescribe a black perspective have a long history of subjugation and subordination. The circumstances that shape a black perspective stem from the experience of racism and powerlessness, both past and present. The motivation that energises a black perspective is rooted to the principle of racial equality and justice.

Keating (2000) reviews the development of black perspectives and their importance in creating a space where black professionals and others could speak and influence social work theory and practice. He identifies three reasons to explain the development of black perspectives. The first reason was to reclaim and recognise the histories, cultures, language, traditions and religions of black people and their relevance for social work. These perspectives addressed forms of marginalisation through recognition and representation of various kinds of knowledge.

The second reason refers to promoting the value of differences and the strengths of black communities in response to the way black families have been pathologised in social work. The third reason refers to the rejection of white norms embedded in histories of racism. This standpoint can promote positive images of black people and provide a political alliance among black people based on experiences of racism.

In many respects, black perspectives have made significant contributions to social work, but Keating (2000) points out the limitations of this approach and in particular its weakness as an all-encapsulating racial definition of people across diverse experiences and situations. This is because racism tends to take on a different appearance in various historical and social contexts. Keating (2000) also raises the issue that black perspectives may promote the idea that the experience of racism is enough to unify black people as a group in their own right. This approach has a tendency to oversimplify and essentialise experiences, rather than acknowledge diverse experiences of racism in various contexts and situations.

Another criticism of black perspectives based on common encounters of racism is that black people's experiences and histories are reduced to their resistance and struggle, which can trivialise black experiences by presenting them simply as a reaction to white domination (Williams, 1999). Here the focus exclusively on oppression as the driving force of black experiences ignores black identities constructed outside the lens of racism and oppression, which suggests black people are solely victims of social circumstances.

It is sometimes argued that using the term 'black' as a fixed category encourages stereotypical ideas about black people and in turn can lead to the view that black cultures are 'innocent' or free from exploitation and oppression. Notwithstanding these concerns, black perspectives not only uncovered contributions to the history and development of social work but also articulated critical writing about lived experiences and alternative sociocultural worldviews. This critical writing can assist in social change because it unsettles familiar social patterns that hold layers of oppressive practices. One of the issues that emerges when anti-racist social work is discarded in favour of an anti-discriminatory framework is that anti-racist social work is likely to be diluted or sidelined so that this perspective in critical practice becomes almost meaningless (Williams, 1999).

Issues of culture in social work

Historically, Britain has always been an ethnically diverse nation. This is an important point to make because many people have been unaware of the historical presence of visible minorities across several centuries and instead have believed that visible minorities are solely migrants who arrived in Britain during the 1950s and 1960s. Dissatisfaction with assimilation policies set the context for multiculturalism as a strategy in educational policies to improve race relations in the 1970s and onwards. These educational policies were closely associated with the process of integration connected to tolerance of cultural diversity as a better way to deal with black and minority pupils. This was followed by the introduction of equal opportunities that featured prominently in official policy (Gillborn, 2001). Many of these strategies adopted cultural products such as music, dance and food to create a multicultural atmosphere in schools. Parents were encouraged to share in these activities and this focus on positive images and the celebration of difference became known as the 3 'S's – saris, samosas and steel bands. Many anti-racist supporters criticised multicultural education as an easy option that created images of exotic cultures but seemed oblivious to the underachievement of black pupils and, equally important, failed to adequately address issues of institutional racism and power.

Similar criticisms about the lack of attention to issues of racism and power followed the development of multicultural perspectives in social work, and preference was given to anti-discriminatory practice as a guide to working with oppressed populations. O'Hagan (2001) argues that social work adopted an anti-culture attitude:

> [Anti-racist and anti-discriminatory practice (ARADP)] … has contributed substantially to the current anti-culture stance of much health and social care literature and practice and has done little to help family and childcare professionals to fulfil the statutory obligations in relation to cultural background and racial origins (1989 Children Act, section 22(5)). (O'Hagan, 2001, p 124)

Following these developments, many people believe that anti-discriminatory practice includes issues of culture that in turn bring cultural sensitivity and competence to practice. However, O'Hagan complains that many people are sadly mistaken because of a focus on structural and local issues of oppression rather than cultural awareness. In light of these criticisms, O'Hagan calls for training in cultural competence not only to counterbalance a preference for models of anti-discriminatory practice but also to maximise the ability of practitioners to engage in cultural competent practice. Multicultural perspectives emphasise the way cultural thinking shapes the way people feel and act so that cultural patterns and norms provide an important context for social work practice.

These perspectives suggest a critical approach because they question social work assumptions that the helping process is free from cultural bias in theory and practice. On the contrary, this profession holds cultural traits and ideology that are often hidden in universal themes and knowledge. One of the problems surrounding the term 'culture' is that there are no standard definitions in social work and this lack of consensus has led to a tendency to oversimplify dimensions of culture and disregard its importance and complexity (O'Hagan, 1999). Social work has looked to other disciplines to get a sense of the breadth of meanings and understandings of culture and relevance for the profession. Definitions of culture have appeared across many fields of study each with their own form and content. This term has an all-embracing meaning but with respect to individuals and families generally covers the way of life, aspects of knowledge and attitudes that are learned and passed down from generation to generation.

As the 1989 Children Act refers to culture and cultural identity as key frames of reference for practice, it is perhaps surprising that little attention has been paid to understanding culture in social work and social care. This is by no means an easy task. Other common definitions of culture refer to "the heritage, traditions, values, attitudes, interpretations and behaviours of a social group or a social group's design for surviving or adapting to its environment" (Banks, 1999a, p 23). This definition, of course, only provides a basic understanding of culture because in real life individuals do not necessarily accept or follow cultural norms or values. This means that people are not exclusively the products of their culture. And in any case most societies have multiple cultures within groups that offer a range of options about accepted cultural norms and values. There are also variations in which cultural norms are internalised into an individual's frame of reference, and thus understanding a group's culture does not provide a roadmap for every situation an individual or family may face (Banks, 1999a). Also, culture norms and values are in a process of constant change as people become geographically mobile and interact with other cultural groups and communities.

As multicultural perspectives in social work have been subject to many criticisms and pitfalls, taking these approaches on board can seem like moving through slippery ice, with the ever-present possibility of 'getting it wrong'. Multicultural perspectives challenge practitioners to think critically about dominant theory and practice frames of reference as well as the cultural identities of service users. Many authors have written about the importance of culture in social work interventions and the need to understand and be sensitive to cultural norms and values in working with individuals and families (Cox and Ephross, 1998; Devore and Schlesinger, 1999; O'Hagan, 1999). There is no doubt that multicultural perspectives have encouraged practitioners to consider differing needs. For example, Meals on Wheels services often did not cater for various dietary needs and as a result distinct cultural needs were not attended to.

Ethnic sensitive approaches have been widely accepted in social work as they focus on practitioner awareness and the need to be 'sensitive' to cultural differences and the value systems of ethnic and cultural groups. In Britain, the term 'ethnicity' is used to refer to minority ethnic groups. This term is employed extensively in social work literature and describes people whose origins are represented as outside of Britain. One problem identified with this term, however, is its tendency to see only certain groups as having 'ethnicity'. This is not the case as all groups in society have ethnicity. Since there is no agreed definition of ethnicity, the term is therefore commonly used to describe differences between groups, for example, a common geographical origin, language, religious faith, shared traditions, values and symbols and cultural features such as literature, music and food (Bowling and Phillips, 2002). These elements are based on the premise that groups are bound together by distinct cultural resources that result in common ways of perceiving and understanding the world.

Although the language of ethnicity has a tendency to position groups outside of mainstream society, it has become popular because it seems to cut across gender and class divisions within groups. Sivanandan (1983) points out that the idea of ethnicity can obscure the social problem of racism and weaken the political voice of black people by framing it into the problem of diverse communities. Despite these ongoing discussions over meanings, problematic, ethnic sensitive approaches have been used by practitioners as a way forward to address the needs of diverse communities. These methods attempt to infuse or adapt social work practice to differing cultural patterns and ways of life, based on the idea that people should be encouraged to retain their cultural heritage, which should be respected and valued.

The interest in multicultural social work has led to the development of cultural competence, which is a popular form of practice in the US.

Models of intervention can be adapted and practice skills adjusted to respond to differing lifestyles and family patterns. This drive for cultural competence recognises the inadequacy of traditional models and the need for improvement and progress. Underlying assumptions in cultural frameworks rely on universal principles that can be applied to many cultural groups, for example, the ability of practitioners to reflect on their own cultural background and biases and how these may impact on relationships with service users. Having knowledge about specific cultural groups is important, particularly past and present experiences of discrimination, but this method gives primacy to a particular approach to practice.

Elsewhere, principally in the US, multiculturalism is commonly an umbrella term that applies to a wide range of approaches, including a critical appraisal of social relations and forms of oppression (Gillborn, 2004). In the social work context, multicultural perspectives support an awareness of and sensitivity to the cultural differences and value systems of ethnic and cultural groups. There are issues of cultural patterns and norms that have received media attention in recent times and some authors attribute dangerous beliefs to particular cultures (O'Hagan, 1999). Although it is important to recognise that no culture is immune to criticism, Corby (1993) and others believe that behavioural explanations are often wrongly interpreted as culture.

As social work has paid little or no attention to issues of culture, it is claimed that the profession has a tendency towards ignorance and indifference towards cultural competence and practice. These issues are often pushed to the outer edges of training and discussion because of the fear of accusations of racism. Some areas of particular concern have been the way women have been subject to long-standing oppressive situations or experiences. Many of these negative or detrimental behaviours appear to be established under the banner of culture rather than issues of power and hierarchical social relations. Some negative behaviours established as cultural 'traditions' have declined over time and this is in part because communities themselves have been engaged in critical dialogue about empowering and disempowering aspects of cultural norms and ways forward for the betterment of individuals and families. Another important dimension to this discussion is cultural identity as a protective and empowering aspect of culture, which is discussed further in Chapter Four.

Anti-racist social work: developing a critical form of practice

Although in recent years there has been a widespread retreat in social work from issues of racism, this form of oppression is central to understanding all kinds of oppressions. Gil (1998, p 13) describes oppression in the following way:"societies are oppressive when people are not considered and treated as equals, and, therefore, do not have equal rights and responsibilities concerning key institutions of social life".The histories of racism in British society are complex and varied, filtered through long periods of enslavement, colonialisation and well-developed racist ideas in academic knowledge and public circles to contemporary forms of exclusion and marginalisation.Although some commentators have challenged the inherent usefulness of the concept of race, because of its historically misleading assumptions about biological differences, this social construct is linked to relations of power and processes of struggle.Van Soest and Garcia (2003) point out:

> 'Race', like gender and sexual orientation, is real in the sense that it has real, though changing effects in the world. It has tangible and complex impacts on people's sense of self, experiences, and life opportunities.Thus, to assert that race and racial difference are socially constructed, is not to minimize their social and political reality. It is, rather, to insist that their reality is precisely social and political rather than inherent and its meaning and function change over time. (Van Soest and Garcia, 2003, p 13)

Because of the profession's direct contact with individuals, many social workers easily adopted a maintenance approach that ensured people coped with or dealt with their problems adequately, thereby helping them adjust to their circumstances.This approach preserves the status quo and some practitioners took the attitude that society was impartial and their role was primarily a practical one that included probing into individuals' and clients' problems in isolation. Any challenges to the social order or 'business as usual' was believed to be contrary to professionalism. These concerns became apparent when many social workers, particularly black social workers, brought issues of racism and sexism to bear on policy and practice in various agencies. Practitioners took an openly political and critical stance, working towards reducing oppression and carrying out practice activities to support social justice.

In a similar vein, radical social work also took a stance against the status quo based on Marxist perspectives (Brake and Bailey, 1980). This approach was critical of individual explanations of clients' problems that had a tendency to blame the victim and seemed indifferent to oppressive social structures and institutions. Brake and Bailey (1980) argued that in order to understand individual problems and circumstances, it is essential to recognise that society has produced long-standing class inequalities that create and contribute to individual difficulties in life. Radical social work was also concerned that social workers were often part of the problem because they supported the status quo often unwittingly, thereby reinforcing social control that was contrary to clients' interests.

In supporting these kinds of practices, social workers were more interested in developing their professional status and standing than seeking alliances with oppressed and marginalised groups. Even though radical social work opened the way for a more progressive position in the profession, its central concern around social class and capitalist arrangements seemed to place issues of race and gender at the margins or to ignore them altogether. These progressive views in social work became increasingly untenable as their weakness was exposed and feminist and anti-racist perspectives began to take hold.

Anti-racist social work emerged in the 1980s as a new form of practice in response to critiques about oppressive tendencies reproduced in and through social work practice (Adams et al, 2002b). These patterns of discrimination produced a contradictory relationship between black communities and social welfare so that black people often experienced minimal access to caring services, yet on the other hand they were inclined to be over-represented in social control aspects of social work such as juvenile justice, mental health units and black children in public care. In particular the negative stereotypes surrounding black families influenced decision-making processes, thus contributing to the high presence of black children in public care. In addition, there appeared to be a lack of motivation to recruit black foster carers and adopters in childcare placements. This is because the selection criteria and norms applied frequently excluded potential black foster carers (Small, 1984).

The lack of attention paid to these issues in policy and practice caused disquiet among black communities and concerned professionals who often felt their concerns were trivialised or not taken seriously by local government authorities. Some community activists suggested that these social work activities were part of a wider agenda of social control eager to remove black children from their families into the care system. In this context, practitioners working in state agencies were seen as part of the problem because black families felt the brunt of the profession's social control responsibilities (Harris, 1991; Graham, 1999).

In order to address these issues, black social workers formed black workers' groups in local authority social services departments to advocate for change in social work institutions. At a local level, these efforts led to the strengthening of anti-racist social work and, in turn, new initiatives in social work education, policy and practice. Alongside these developments, social workers recognised the need for a national association and in 1983 the Association of Black Social Workers and Allied Professions was created. This professional organisation became responsible for establishing anti-racist social work as a critical framework for practice and support networks under the leadership of John Small, Gloria Barnes and others. It played a major role in shifting the ideological base of social work as well as shaping legislative arrangements to address the needs of black children and their families.

Growing anxieties inside and outside the profession about insensitive forms of practice with black families hastened calls for a re-examination of social work priorities. As these issues were debated, social work began to acknowledge that the profession must change and realign itself with oppressed populations in a practical way (Dominelli, 1988; Ahmad, 1990; Turney, 1996). This repositioning of social work is identified by Adams et al (2002a, p 5), who believe that social workers should:

> ... engage in progressive practice which takes the side of people who have been subjugated by structural inequalities such as poverty, sexism and racism and seeks to assist them in their desire to reverse the position they are in, that is, to move in emancipatory directions.

Through this shift in social work thinking, practitioners were no longer locked into class as a major social division. Instead, first race and gender were taken on board as sources of inequalities and then, later, disability, gay and lesbian issues, and ageing. These structural explanations moved social work practice away from traditional assumptions that tended to blame individuals for social problems, and in their place a recasting of social work acknowledged a measured understanding of discrimination in society. Dominelli (1988) and others proposed a model of anti-racist social work that considered an evaluation of society from the standpoint of marginalised groups as a key principle in critical theory and practice. Taking this approach, it is possible to understand how

---

systems of oppression shape the life experiences of those service users who belong to marginalised groups.

Dominelli (1988) begins by identifying several aspects of racism in social work that need to be addressed in order to establish anti-racist practices. These elements cover three main areas:

1. Individual prejudices, biases and stereotypes.
2. Institutional racism.
3. Cultural racism.

Using these elements of anti-racist practice, Dominelli (1988) first applies the strategies and approaches used by social workers to avoid dealing with racism in the first place:

- A denial that racism exists particularly in its cultural or institutional forms. Social workers using this strategy see racism as nothing more than personal prejudice confined to a few extreme individuals.
- Experiences of everyday racism are not recognised or acknowledged and issues of racism are perceived as irrelevant in most situations.
- The acceptance of racism in countries such as the US or South Africa but a refusal to accept that racism permeates British society.
- Colour-blind strategies based on theories of assimilation that perceive race and discrimination as insignificant.
- A patronising approach to black people that operates through a superficial acceptance of cultural values and differences that are tolerated within a context of an inferiority and deficit model.
- Dumping strategies that regard racism as a problem for black people and therefore they alone should be engaged in challenging racist practices.
- Avoidance strategies based on the idea that racism exists but shying away from opportunities to do something about it.

By bringing together common strategies working across social work institutions and practice, Dominelli's model moved the issues of racism and discrimination to the centre of debate in the profession. These concerns resulted in not only increasing awareness of racism and discrimination among practitioners but also served to bring about new initiatives in social work education, namely Paper 30 (CCETSW, 1989).

Doing anti-racist social work

Even though social workers are concerned with people who experience oppression and attempt to deal with issues of oppression, social work itself can be oppressive in its own right. Therefore it is essential to think critically about designing social work interventions and all aspects of practice. Anti-racist social work is constructed on several basic principles that inform social work models for practice. These are described in the following way:

1. Anti-racist social work recognises that 'race' is a social construct that involves social and political meanings and has been used to justify and encourage differential treatment and oppression.
2. Anti-racist social work critically examines the dynamics of power relationships and institutional racism that produces racial and gender sources of oppression.
3. Anti-racist social work considers that the full social effects of racism cannot be understood without understanding other forms of oppression.
4. Anti-racist social work entails self-awareness of prejudices, biases and stereotypes in individual interpersonal relationships.
5. Anti-racist practice promotes a working knowledge of the interlocking nature of oppression as a tool for social change.
6. Anti-racist practice includes black perspectives, worldviews and lived experiences of oppression in a working partnership with service users.

As anti-racist social work consists of working across individual, agency and structural levels, this process starts with self-awareness of one's own values and prejudices, and critical thinking about how actions can reproduce structures of oppression. In developing this overview, practitioners recognise that race matters in social relations and critical practice begins with reflecting on one's own personal experiences, history and social practice. As Van Soest and Garcia (2003) maintain, issues of oppression include everyone in the equation, those who are marginalised as well as those who benefit from oppression.

The idea of benefiting from oppression has often been sidelined in favour of concentrating on those on the receiving end of oppression. But there is another side to oppression that uncovers the ways in which groups in society have social arrangements of advantage. These arrangements are embedded in the unmarked and unnamed status of the majority society as the norm and therefore become invisible (Van

Soest and Garcia, 2003).This means that self-awareness of practitioners becomes critical in unpacking these issues as well as a willingness to work with the consequences of biases even if applied unwittingly. By thinking in a critical way about social inequalities, it is possible to construct a social work that works for greater social justice and human betterment.

Since its beginnings, the term 'anti-racism' has been subject to critique and sometimes ridicule, particularly from conservative circles. It is often the case that many terms in the social sciences are disputed, and, in this case, anti-racism has had its fair share of disagreements. Some of these discussions have centred on the word 'racism' and its association with old ideas of 'race' as marking out misleading differences between groups of people. However, numerous writers argue that many people continue to believe that race is real and that this belief has real consequences (Pilkington, 2003). Hopton (1997) considers that this focus on language forms diverts attention away from attempts to eliminate discrimination and to empower members of minority groups. Using other language forms marginalises the lived experiences of visible minority groups and tends to reconfigure issues of racism as cultural difference or individual differences that play down general patterns of disadvantage. Many critics of anti-racism have often dubbed this term and its practices as nothing more than 'political correctness'.

Nevertheless, Dei (2005) insists that anti-racism is more than discussions about its meanings; it is a form of critical theory that opposes race-based power dynamics that already affect the lives of too many. Anti-racist social work also means learning about the lived experiences of those who are marginalised to maximise partnerships and to think about this form of practice as a vehicle for social change. Over time those groups who have been excluded along the lines of race, gender and class have resisted the way society operates to organise towards social change.

Social change often comes about when inconsistencies and long-standing forms of injustice can no longer be denied or avoided. For example, in recent years, there has been much discussion and media attention concerning racial hate crimes. Much of the motivation behind the 2000 Race Relations (Amendment) Act has been the brutal killing of Stephen Lawrence, a college student stabbed to death while waiting for a bus on his way home. The lengthy struggles of the Lawrence family and concerned individuals for justice culminated in widespread recognition of institutional racism in public services. Although black communities have been speaking about the ways in which racism permeates Britain's structures and institutions for many years, it was this tragic event that galvanised public concern to take the matter seriously.

The lack of professional care identified in the subsequent Macpherson Inquiry (1999, para 0.34) provides a stark example of institutional racism and its prevalence in British society. The report points to the "collective failure of a [public service] organisation to provide appropriate and professional services to people because of their colour, culture, or ethnic origin. It can be seen or detected in processes, attitudes and behaviour which amount to discrimination through unwitting prejudice, ignorance, thoughtlessness and racist stereotyping which disadvantage minority ethnic people". For the first time the 2000 Race Relations (Amendment) Act brings anti-discriminatory principles to bear on public services, including social services. Local authorities are now charged with promoting racial equality and an obligation to provide appropriate services. It is still early days to assess whether this legislation has been implemented in the way it was intended.

In a recent qualitative study (Forbat, 2004) participants were invited to talk about their experiences of looking after a relative with dementia or their own experiences of having dementia. They were also asked to comment on their interactions with statutory agencies. A service user from an Indian background commented on the lack of support from social services:

> I do feel bitter about it because I think people like my Mum are being abused. I mean she's been here since 1964 not once has she claimed a penny. Dad was too proud to claim for anything. She could have been sitting at home and claiming. Dad never let her, he provided for us right and he never took a day off, he went to work, came home had a stroke and was bedridden from then on. Mum looked after him twenty two, twenty years. (Forbat, 2004, p 320)

As Forbat (2004) explains in this extract, the service user labels this interaction with local services as 'racist'. She understands this interaction through ideas of residency which have been used historically to deny services to black and minority people. These actions were applied to determine whether her parents were deserving of services. Forbat (2004) concludes by calling for social action to put ideas into practice and working more effectively across dimensions of difference.

Conclusion

This chapter has considered anti-racist social work as the leading model of practice in bringing issues of racism and discrimination into the profession. One of its important contributions was to shift thinking away from notions of tolerance of black communities towards issues of power and domination. These issues provided a starting framework that established anti-racist principles in theory and practice. By focusing on issues of racism a working knowledge of the social constraints and effects of discrimination emerged as central to social work practice. This has been achieved within the context of powerful state-managed bureaucracies and some resistance in institutions of higher learning. One of the strengths of anti-racist social work that is often overlooked is its potential is to give voice to black perspectives and understandings about the way social problems are understood and possible solutions or ways forward. These critical voices are often pushed to the margins, as the views of black service users fade into the background in the quagmire of bureaucratic practices.

Williams (1999) laments the demise of anti-racist social work because despite its important contributions it appeared to be a 'fashionable blip' in social work history. In making connections with wider issues of oppression, anti-racist social work has been subject to a weakening of its development as well as a loss of commitment to these issues in social work generally, in favour of equal opportunities and diversity. Black perspectives have struggled to retain some footing in the era of anti-oppressive practice. This has been difficult given the mechanisms of silencing and marginalisation operating in British institutions including social work education and society generally. In the current climate, it is easy to lose sight of anti-racist social work as a strategy for social change as well as bringing recognition and presence to those visible minorities who often experience the brunt of discrimination and unfairness in British society.

THREE

Rethinking oppression and social divisions

Introduction

As anti-racist social work gained ground among many practitioners, its limitations began to surface. Although this approach established a central place for issues of oppression in social work, this form of practice was perceived as too narrow and seemed to neglect other forms of oppression and discrimination. Against this background, anti-discriminatory practice became an umbrella term to describe various sources and forms of oppression that interact with each other and reflect social divisions of class, race, gender, age, disability and sexual identity (Thompson, 1993). This framework developed by drawing on literature that presented a comprehensive understanding of social divisions in society. For example, new theories and critical thinking about disability emerged from disability movements and the voices of people with disabilities themselves. This underpinning knowledge, gathered largely from sociology, was harnessed by social work to ensure practice was well informed. In a similar vein, practitioners were encouraged to maximise partnerships with clients and to engage their experiences and understandings in framing interventions. The notion of empowerment, even with its numerous meanings and lack of consensus among practitioners, encapsulates this thinking.

This chapter begins by exploring the different ways oppression operates as a set of processes that result in direct and indirect forms of discrimination. Following these issues, the next section opens with a brief account of anti-discriminatory practice and anti-oppressive practice. These terms are often used interchangeably and there appears to be some confusion about their meanings that seems to be associated with different underpinning approaches. The section attempts to clarify and untangle these closely related terms to present a clearer picture for practice. Beyond the basic models of anti-discriminatory practice, several social work authors have tried to integrate more complex understandings of social divisions and power into models of practice (Adams et al, 2002b; Dominelli, 2002). These more in-depth understandings of oppression have emerged in recent years as marginalised groups have brought their perspectives into social work. In another way, postmodern perspectives have called for a more sophisticated understanding of power and oppression and this chapter looks at these theories as a particular view of knowledge. Postmodern perspectives have raised questions about some aspects of theories about racism and black perspectives generally. So, although postmodern theories have assisted in bringing the voices of marginalised groups into view, they have also diminished concern about the collective experiences and histories of black communities in favour of identities. Several black perspectives are explored in the second half of the chapter, including other developments that have emerged: a rethinking about issues of power, and a growing interest in white privilege and in diversity as the new language of equal opportunities. These areas are looked at in relation to social work and social care.

This chapter aims to explore the broader aspects of oppression that include issues of diversity, difference and operations of power. Many of these contemporary issues and debates about social divisions are connected to postmodern social theory that has influenced the field of social work.

Understanding models of oppression

Models of anti-discriminatory and anti-oppressive practice have become the mainstay of social work education as new students to the profession seek to promote equality as a basic requirement of good practice. To apply these models of practice it is necessary to have an understanding of oppression, its various features and the ways it can operate in society. A working knowledge of oppression includes issues of power and social injustice. By making the case that issues of justice are beyond the distribution of rewards, opportunities and social goods, it is possible to uncover the constraints of institutional conditions to make sense of the social experiences of marginalised groups (Young, 1990). As anti-discriminatory practice has developed, simplistic thinking about oppression has been replaced by explanations that acknowledge its complexity in various situations and contexts.

It has long been recognised that levels of oppression and their intensity vary among societies. These differ in degrees of inequality and are reflected in the social institutions of daily life that impact on individuals and families. The concept of oppression can best be understood as relational, that is, it is embedded in the relationships that exist between individuals, social groups or between entire societies

(Mullaly, 2001). The relationship between discrimination and oppression is complex and apparent in multiple levels of social interaction. One way to approach this relationship is to understand the extent to which the different features of oppression are interconnected. These connections produce a set of processes by which certain groups are discriminated against across structural, social and political areas of society. They are the source of oppression that in turn sets off direct and indirect forms of discrimination (Thompson, 1997).

In trying to unravel these complex forms of oppression operating in society, Young's (1990) model of oppression is a useful starting point. Young describes five forms of oppression: marginalisation, exploitation, powerlessness, cultural imperialism and violence. According to Young (1990) it is not possible to find a common description or essential cause of oppression because social groups experience oppression to varying degrees and in different ways. In taking these issues on board and to avoid disputes about whose oppression is more severe, it is more useful to think about these forms of oppression as sets of conditions as well as sets of ideas. In this respect, all oppressed people experience similar conditions.

Young (1990) breaks down the idea that oppression means that there is a single oppressor or oppressing group, and instead sees oppression as fluctuating and changeable. Although structural oppression involves social relations among groups, it is also necessary to look at the way power operates as people are going about their everyday lives. For example, although the roots of racism in Britain cannot be understood without understanding the history of enslavement and empire, Bhavnani et al (2005) maintain that it is necessary to explore the context in which racism is reproduced in society on a daily basis. Two categories of racism stand out: first, 'elite racism' refers to racism reproduced at a national level through the media, the government and other influential figures. Racism such as this is often unchallenged and is expressed as the 'norm', forming part of public perceptions. This kind of racism results in misinformation and sanctions negative representations of black individuals and communities. The second type of racism is referred to as 'situated racism'. This category of racism is concerned with localised experiences at the micro-level and refers to individual experiences of unequal treatment. These two explanations of racism in specific contexts show how patterns of behaviour are ingrained in both 'macro' and 'micro' social structures and underpin everyday aspects of British culture. By considering attitudes and ideas that have historically subordinated certain groups, it is possible to discern the ways social divisions are embedded in the development of British society (Bhavnani et al, 2005).

These more complex characteristics of oppression are important for social workers in order to fully understand the social conditions of marginalised groups that impede their full participation in society. Young's (1990) five categories of oppression can be used to determine the degree of vulnerability groups may experience:

- *Marginalisation*: this form of oppression has severe consequences because it pushes groups to the outer edges of society and they are made to feel invisible or experience lack of recognition. Groups vulnerable to marginalisation experience not only material deprivation but also exclusion due to their marginal status. For example, black communities experience marginal status particularly in the public sphere where their perspectives or worldviews about social issues are denied or ignored. This kind of oppression is also experienced by other social groups, such as older people and people with disabilities, where social arrangements and structures tend to block opportunities for participation and which in turn perpetuates lack of recognition and respect.
- *Powerlessness*: the issue of power underpins most models of oppression and this subject has been examined in many ways to ascertain its relationship to inequality and discrimination. Power is a feature of modern social life and is observed as some groups in society have more authority or influence than others. Power is best understood as a form of social relations where inequalities lead to forms of oppression.
- *Violence*: many marginalised groups in society suffer violence. This means unprovoked attacks, threats of violence or incidents of harassment. For Young (1990) violence is a social practice and social groups who are targets of 'hate' crimes live under threat of harassment and violence.
- *Cultural imperialism*: less attention has been devoted to this form of oppression. When a dominant group's experiences and culture are highly visible and reinforced on a daily basis through the media, institutions and other forms of social interaction, they become established as the norm. Dominant groups in society have access to means of communication in society and, therefore, they can express the experiences, values and achievements of that group. As Young (1990) maintains, dominant groups can project their own experiences as representative of humanity. These measures are reinforced so that the dominant group can maintain its position and

marginalised groups are constructed as 'the other' in stereotypical ways. This process means that marginalised groups are often marked out by stereotypes in public representations or everyday encounters. At the same time, this process relegates marginalised groups' experiences and perspectives in life as irrelevant, finding little expression that touches the dominant group. For example, the contribution of black people and their histories to social welfare and social work has largely been ignored or seen as irrelevant to the development of social work. In a similar fashion, the worldviews and interpretations of social life of marginalised groups often lack public recognition.

- *Exploitation*: this form of oppression relates to societies divided by social class. The term 'social class' has been subject to many debates, which has led to a decline in its importance as a tool of analysis. Until recently, social class was seen as a major social division and the source of material inequalities. Marxists use the concept of exploitation to explain the workings of the capitalist system that allows the upper classes to amass enormous wealth at the expense of the working classes. Those from working-class backgrounds often face periods of unemployment and poverty and are more likely to suffer from ill health. This is because working-class people are subject to social rules about what work is and receive compensation for part of their labour, the surplus being retained as profit for the employer. In capitalist societies there is a distinct form of social relations that allows for some people to accumulate material goods while it also constrains many more. From this perspective, exploitation is a feature of capitalism and is implicated in creating social problems including poverty, exclusion and inequality.

Racists axe black teenager to death

Tracy McVeigh and Amelia Hill
Sunday, 31 July 2005
The Observer

A gang of men who murdered a black teenager with an axe in an unprovoked racist attack in a park near his home in Huyton, Liverpool, were being hunted by police last night.

Anthony Walker, an 18-year-old sixth form college student, was killed by a single blow delivered with such force that the axe was left embedded in his forehead.

Just minutes before the attack the teenager, his girlfriend and his cousin had been subjected to a 'torrent of racial abuse' by a man in a hooded top.

Detective Chief Superintendent Peter Currie, who is leading the inquiry, said Anthony had spent the evening at home with his girlfriend, who is white and a fellow student at college in Huyton.

Shortly before 11.30pm, they walked to the bus stop outside the Huyton Park pub on St Johns Road so that Anthony's girlfriend could get a 10 minute bus ride home to Kirkby.

But as they waited with Anthony's male cousin, who is also black, they were racially abused by the man, who was standing outside the pub. They left to find another bus stop because they 'didn't want any bother or trouble'.

But minutes later, as they walked through the park, they were attacked by three or four men and Anthony was dead.

Bernard Lawson, Assistant Chief Constable of Merseyside, said: "Our first thoughts go out to his family and we have met his mother and his sister and they are bearing up tremendously."

"Anthony was a young Christian studying for his A-levels and wanting to be a lawyer. Those dreams for him and his family are now dashed."

Anthony's girlfriend and cousin saw him hit and ran to get help. Minutes later they returned to find him slumped on the ground with the axe embedded in his head.

He was taken to Whiston hospital before being transferred to Walton Neurological Centre, where he died at 5.25 yesterday morning.

Lawson said that there had been a number of other incidents of racial abuse in the area in recent weeks and appealed for local people to come forward with information on the attack.

Source: McVeigh and Hill (2005)

Moving to anti-discriminatory practice

Models of anti-discriminatory practice have become accepted forms of intervention in social work education and practice. Thompson (1997, p 33) describes anti-discriminatory practice as an approach to social work that attempts to reduce, undermine or eliminate forms of discrimination and oppression. Social workers deal with people who experience discrimination and this approach to social work recognises that it is more than an individual experience and instead takes on board that certain sections of the population experience discrimination of various forms in society.

It should be apparent by now that social work and its institutions also operate in oppressive ways. Social workers occupy influential positions and there is considerable scope for oppressive kinds of practice to take place. This increased awareness about forms of discrimination within social work as well as in society generally has enabled practitioners to see individuals in their social context. In order to apply anti-discriminatory approaches to practice, social workers need a working knowledge of discrimination and oppression including the possibility of discrimination in their own practice. Thompson (1997) advocates for justice, equality and participation as the three important interacting elements of practice.

What does anti-discriminatory practice involve?

- By understanding the ways discrimination can occur and its likely impact on clients and communities, practitioners can develop a working knowledge of discrimination as the basis for developing skills for practice.
- Challenging discriminatory behaviour and practice.
- Valuing diversity.
- Commitment to social justice, equality and participation.

Thompson (1997) outlines an anti-discriminatory model of social work by examining the social circumstances of clients on three levels. These three levels are referred to as a PCS analysis. The first level is described as personal or psychological because this level is concerned with thoughts, feelings, attitudes and action. This level can also refer to the interaction between practitioners and clients, that is, practice, and, lastly, prejudice, defined as the inflexibility of the mind. This level takes place in the context of culture that is the next level of examination in this model. Culture refers to cultural understandings, shared ways of seeing, values and patterns of thought and behaviour. Another important dimension of this level is an assumed consensus of normality that produces conformity to social norms. These elements come together as a vehicle for conveying and reinforcing this culture. The final level refers to the structural levels of society and the network of social divisions that are closely linked to power relations. Thompson (1997) avoids the pitfall of separating these levels as single units by blending them into interlocking patterns of power and influence. The PCS levels offer a model that understands social divisions across and through individual, cultural and structural dimensions and how these levels maintain and reinforce each other. Because this model takes individual, cultural and structural forces into understanding discrimination, then it follows that approaches that stop short at individual explanations are clearly inadequate.

Anti-oppressive practice

As anti-discriminatory practice became established as the primary model or approach to social work practice, other writers have suggested that discrimination is only one area of oppression that is situated in social relations (Healy, 2000; Mullaly, 2001). Moreover, the concentrated focus on discrimination seemed inadequate to challenge power differences among social groups in society. Thus, anti-oppressive practice is concerned with structural forces and social relations between groups in society. Dominelli (2002, p 8) explains oppression in this way:

> ... oppression involves relations of domination that divide people into dominant or superior groups and subordinate or inferior ones. These relations of domination consist of the systematic devaluing of the attributes and contributions of those deemed inferior.

Dominelli (2002a) places the dynamics of oppression in the social arena in the form of interactions between people. To understand oppression in all its forms, it is necessary to see oppression as not just 'out there' in an abstract form but as a general experience that informs every aspect of people's lives, from psychological devaluation of personhood to social, political and economic injustice. In an earlier section, several kinds of oppression in modern society were outlined that seemed to be neglected in the literature dealing with oppression. From this point of view, oppression can be seen as a web of interconnecting processes operating in different situations and contexts. If this is the case, how can practitioners best understand its complexities to avoid and uncover oppressive practices? Perhaps a good start would be to give a brief outline of anti-oppression as an umbrella term for critical perspectives in social work that have a number of things in common.

In the history of social work, critical traditions hold a central place in developing forms of critical practice. In order to achieve social justice and equality it is necessary to draw on the insights of a range of critical theories such as feminism and anti-racist approaches. These perspectives propose wider examination of social divisions to bring about change in social relations and create a better world. In order to realise these possibilities, social workers need to widen the boundaries of concern to contribute to changes in social, political and economic structures (Hick et al, 2005).

Common themes of anti-oppressive practice

- An understanding that social and personal issues social workers deal with on a daily basis cannot be understood or dealt with apart from their social and political causes.
- Self-reflection and a critical stance are required to make sense of the contradictory effects of social work practice and social policies.
- Participatory approaches are promoted rather than authoritarian practice relations.
- Commitment to work with and for oppressed populations to achieve social justice.
- Social work can perpetuate social problems.

Source: Adapted from Healy (2001)

Healy (2001) brings together critical theories and postmodern understandings to reinvigorate critical social practice in the context of social changes that have taken place over the past four decades. The rise of globalisation, market-driven approaches to social services and widespread inequalities indicate an increasing need for critically oriented practice in social work.

There are diverse opinions about which perspectives can be embraced as the 'correct' or better way to engage in forms of critical practice. This might be because each perspective is dealing with a different area of social life and in any case all are drawn from different points of view. Healy (2001) believes that theory often fails to speak to the concerns of practice. This situation is no different from other human service disciplines such as teaching and nursing. Although many practitioners are committed to critical practice, they are sometimes reluctant to engage with theory because they do not see how it can enable them to better understand and develop their practice. These challenges have become more apparent in a climate where social control functions in social work have increased regulation of social work activities.

Healy (2001) advocates that theory should be recognised as a resource rather than as a blueprint for practice in acknowledging the limits of theory for guiding practice. Healy also points out that "critical practice ideals have the potential to do good and to do harm; the critical practice literature has paid too little attention to the negative outcomes of critical practice principles" (Healy, 2001, p 16).

Payne (2005) outlines some of the criticisms of critical social work practice:

- There are tensions between dealing with individual issues and problems while at the same time addressing social inequalities in the broader society. Critical theory seems to neglect the immediate personal needs of clients.
- Critical theory does not seem to attend to emotional issues and many of the problems that clients present, and offers little in terms of guidelines for practice, although radical perspectives do allow for clients' voices to be heard and responded to, particularly marginalised and excluded voices.
- This form of practice often fails to engage in a complex understanding of power and how it equates with control. Many critiques maintain that even victimised clients have power in some contexts and situations.
- Critical social work does not deal with religious oppression and human rights abuses that have become important issues for practitioners.

Even though many of these criticisms have valid points, critical theories offer a useful perspective of contemporary society and offer an examination of social issues to help social workers to think creatively about their practice (Payne, 2005).

The focus of critical practice remains strongly aligned to structural forces, institutions and social arrangements in society. In mapping out the streams of critical social work practice, it is necessary to have some understanding of the main elements that underpin an approach to this kind of practice. Postmodern theories continue to influence critical forms of practice because these theories attempt to explain the implications of rapid social change in society. As social work 'borrows' knowledge from a number of disciplines, and in particular sociology, new theories about the nature of society and the relationship between the individual and the social world influence and shape the profession's intellectual heritage and development of practice.

Postmodern theories

Postmodern theory is a way of understanding the social world and emerged as a critique of modernism and the Enlightenment philosophies that perceived universal knowledge developed through the use of scientific methods as the key to human progress in society. It is claimed that social work is a product of modernism because it is based on the idea that by studying and understanding social problems, rational action can be taken to deal with them. Postmodern social theory has revealed some important issues about the ways in which societies are changing. This form of social theory has had a significant influence on the social sciences generally, leading to a rethinking about social arrangements in everyday life and new areas of study.

Several authors have discussed the difficulty in defining and grasping the main principles of postmodern social theory because it appears to be a slippery concept that attempts to understand and respond to the complexities of social life. Thus, it is difficult to capture universal features of this social theory because this perspective rejects this kind of thinking and instead proposes that society is characterised by social change, complexity and ambiguity (Alvesson, 2002).

As social change has become a common feature in everyday modern life, many commentators have suggested that these changes cannot be explained by traditional approaches such as Marxism and feminism that seemed to work in previous eras. It is often argued that the traditional boundaries between social groups are breaking down and it is more difficult in contemporary society to predict the lifestyles that people will adopt. For example, it is argued that class no longer influences people in the way that it used to, and therefore class as a generalised theory is less able to explain human behaviour in contemporary society. Just as class tended to be presented as a general theory of differences between social groups, feminism seemed to present women as a homogeneous group with little emphasis on differences of histories and experiences between women and within categories of women. Postmodernism emphasises differences between people and social groups rather than similarities and generalisations.

According to Beck (1998), people are coming to think of themselves as unique individuals who have chosen their identities and are no longer bound to family or class in the traditional way. These changes have happened because of new social processes such as consumerism, which shifted traditional fixed positions in society. This perspective involves recognising different points of view as equally valid and promoting the voices of groups excluded on the basis of gender, race and class. In keeping with these developments, postmodern perspectives attach importance to knowledge and particularly the use of language that expresses points of view that can never be proved to be correct or absolute truth. Meanings and realities are constructed out of language and collections of ideas about human action and behaviour. This means language and meaning must be explained in relation to its social context that may be historical, social and political (Fook, 2002).

These features of postmodern thought challenge ideas about knowledge as neutral and instead claim knowledge is best understood as a form of power that is specific to particular historical periods and social contexts. These concerns are important to social work because the profession is built on general universal knowledge that can be applied to many situations in practice. By examining the way knowledge for social work is constructed, it is possible to identify the taken for granted hierarchies and norms that exist and provide alternative ways to value marginalised voices and lived experiences as ways of knowing and making sense of the world.

Postmodern perspectives are critical of the helping professions including social work because professions are perceived as social control agents involved in relations of surveillance and disciplining social groups who are seen as 'deviant' or marginalised and on the outer edges of society. It is claimed that the pace of social change in society has created a sense of uncertainty for many people, and issues of risk have emerged, attracting attention in public and academic circles. Historically, social work has been preoccupied with the morality of clients but shifts in social and economic factors and changes in the profession have caused practitioners to be more concerned with managing risk behaviour (Reamer, 1998).

In the wake of postmodern influences, the traditional boundaries between fields of study have started to break down. For example, in recent years sociology and cultural studies have come together to develop new areas of research and interest. Sociology has developed a renewed interest in the body as a way of understanding social relationships and identity. The body as a social entity in its own right was hidden from view and subject to biological and social investigation in isolation across several disciplines. However, this new area of study brings together the body's physical, social and psychological nature in understanding life experiences.

Having outlined some of the themes of postmodern thinking, there are some identifiable strands that seem to run through this theoretical framework (Alvesson, 2002):

- the centrality of language as a set of ideas
- fragmented identities
- loss of foundations and the power of general universal theories
- connections between knowledge and power.

With the introduction of postmodern perspectives, social work has been somewhat reluctant to engage with postmodern theories. This may be because these perspectives challenge ideas of professionalism and the distancing of client and social worker that are implicated in power relations. Moreover, social work finds it difficult to deal with uncertainty, ambiguity and complexity given its historical development based on universal methods and applications. These concerns have stimulated long-standing debates about what kind of knowledge is required for social work and social care, and, moreover, the best way to assess the quality of underpinning knowledge together with potential for uptake in practice.

In an attempt to bring together multiple knowledge sources, professional bodies such as the Social Care Institute for Excellence (SCIE) have developed a classification system for social care knowledge. This framework provides standards to assess the quality of knowledge in order to develop a model of 'professional knowledge'. The SCIE identify five sources of knowledge in social care:

- Organisational: knowledge gained from the management and governance of social care.
- Practitioner: knowledge gained from the conduct of social care.
- Policy: community knowledge gained from the wider policy environment.
- Research: knowledge gathered systematically with predetermined design.
- User: knowledge gained from experience of service use and reflection thereon (Pawson et al, 2003).

Given the complexity and increasing sources of knowledge about social life, setting out guidelines to identify suitable knowledge for social work and social care is a challenging and difficult task. Long et al (2006) correctly point out that social workers need a more reflective and critical stance towards information arising from the diverse sources of knowledge.

Although postmodern theories have brought into view issues of ambiguity and complexity in social work, some authors have found aspects of these theories relevant for practice. Fook (2002) summarises key ways these perspectives can lead to more flexibility and possibilities for social work practice:

- The focus on social context and its links with individual experiences can provide understanding of the individual in various social contexts. This is important because it helps to develop understanding of how the social structure is part of everyday experience.
- The recognition of multiple perspectives and complexity to both issues and solutions that confront social workers should allow for more effective practice.
- An allowance for changing identities and flexibility because living in contemporary society is mediated by social context.
- An understanding of how knowledge for social work is constructed and produced can open up alternative ways to value the voices of clients.
- The critique of mainstream practices can upend power differences and allow for new forms of empowerment (adapted from Fook, 2002).

As postmodern theories have gained currency across many disciplines, concern has been noted about how multiple sources of knowledge have informed and influenced social work and social care.

Black perspectives and postmodern theories

There has been some discussion among black scholars about the way postmodern perspectives have emerged and the significant influence of these theories in the social sciences generally, including the field of social work. According to Gordon (1995), one of the factors involved in the shift towards postmodern social theory has been the decline of European cultural dominance posed by black civil rights, anti-colonial and feminist movements. Postmodern thinking with its focus on new identities, otherness, resistance and diversity on the one hand opens up opportunities for marginalised groups to be heard. Yet at the same time, it tends to suppress collective histories and experiences that are often the building blocks of shared identities and accounts of long-standing social oppressions. Because of this process, postmodern theories seem to elevate individualism, which can in turn act as a way of silencing oppressed groups by undermining their collective efforts to seek social justice and recognition.

Gordon (1995) agrees with this point and sees this intellectual movement as underestimating the social realities of racism that confront black communities. These concrete political, economic and social realities fly in the face of postmodernist responses that tend to shy away from structural constraints and instead shift attention to imaginative texts and narratives. Leaving these criticisms aside, postmodern thinking has made important inroads not only in uncovering the linkages between power and knowledge as a mechanism of domination, but also in refining black perspectives to take account of the complexity of racisms and the interlocking nature of social oppression, particularly in the area of gender and race. Postmodern thought has also assisted in giving voice to marginalised perspectives, albeit in a limited way. It is useful at this point to briefly outline several black perspectives based on different but distinct orientations. While these orientations have their particular interests and viewpoints may differ, they write from a unique angle on self, community and society.

Theories about issues of race and inequalities

Issues of discrimination and inequality have been the subject of research and debate for many years. The much quoted words by W.E.B. DuBois (1903, p 13), that "the problem of the twentieth century is the problem of the 'color-line'", encapsulates this ongoing social problem in society. Early developments on this subject tended to focus on the problems of assimilation into the majority society and individual attitudes and prejudice. For many decades now, black intellectuals in the US have developed Black, African American and Africana Studies as an interdisciplinary field that seeks to bring about the critical study of the multidimensional aspects of people who identify or define themselves as black. In the UK, there are a growing number of black and minority scholars developing the field, bringing a unique view of a colonial background to this arena.

Some of the theories about race inequalities have attempted to unravel questions about the significance of race and class and its relevance to the understanding of social oppression. Black scholarly works, such as Eric Williams' *Capitalism and slavery* (1964) and, two decades later, William Julius Wilson's *The declining significance of race* (1980), emphasise class as the basis for understanding discrimination and exploitation of black people in western societies. For these writers, class is just as important as race in the process of creating social inequalities. Capitalism is a key factor in creating and reproducing racism as a by-product of class oppression, and, therefore, is integral to capitalist structures and operations (Christian, 2004). A group of black academics at the Centre for Contemporary Cultural Studies (CCCS) in Birmingham examined race and ethnicity in their own social contexts, including the construction of race as a political issue, which provided a more rounded understanding of the extent of racial discrimination in society (CCCS, 1982).

Another important theory about racism has been developed by Essed (1991). This work presents a new approach to understanding racism and looks at its pervasive impact on the daily experiences of black people. Essed (1991) argues that the concept of everyday racism is useful in showing that racism is reproduced largely through routine and taken-for-granted social practices in everyday life. This does not mean that this informal kind of racism is relatively harmless; on the contrary these day-to-day injustices can have an adverse effect on mental and physical health. The day-to-day realities of racism in the lives of black people do not often receive much attention, and Essed (1991) considers that these experiences are important for demonstrating how multidimensional aspects of racism come together and operate simultaneously.

Essed (1991) believes that black people can develop sophisticated knowledge about the reproduction of racism in everyday life and through these experiences new sets of meanings can be revealed. This work also identified the way in which racisms are gendered and have entered understandings of black men and women emerging in different social practices and impacts. For example, black and minority ethnic women are often deemed more suitable for jobs on the lowest rung of the labour market within an area already segregated by gender.

Graham and Robinson's (2004) study discusses gendered racism in connection with the experiences of black boys in the British educational system. There is a legacy of historical and social constructions of black men in which they are often demonised or positioned as a threat to the majority society. These stereotypes and public representations come together with constructions of masculinity so that the process of racism manifests itself in gendered ways. For example, Mark, a 13-year-old boy, is acutely aware of racial stereotypes infused into social practices shaping his daily social realities. He says:

> We can't change it. When you get a cab they ask for the
> money first. When you walk past a white person in a car
> they lock their doors. I hate it when you walk past a white

lady in the street and she starts clutching her bag. Go into the shops, and they follow you. They think bad about us because they think we black people have no brains – they think all black people are the same – they think every black person is a criminal. (Cited in Graham and Robinson, 2004, p 663)

In presenting or examining racism in this way, social workers can fully appreciate the way representations are played out in everyday social realities and the impact of these experiences on the well-being of black people generally.

Theories about race and gender: black feminist thought

The issues of race and gender have attracted much attention over the years and were often examined largely as separate entities rather than connected forms of oppression. Black feminists raised concerns about the lack of attention among feminists to racism and the specific forms of oppression faced by black women. For example, black writers criticised feminists for producing literature written by and for white women (Carby, 1982; hooks, 1984). Black women were largely absent from feminist writings and emerging theories about a range of women's concerns. Black women were 'invisible' in the early development of Women's Studies in the same fashion as feminists claimed women were in waves of critiques about the male-dominated examination of social life.

By becoming informed about marginalised women and their social experiences it became clear that gender inequality could no longer be articulated in a straightforward way. The idea of 'woman' as a universal category was called into question as differences between women, including their experiences of oppression, began to surface and demand attention. Many black women distanced themselves from feminism because these perspectives tended to take little account of the experience of black communities or the histories of racial discrimination. Carby (1982, p 25) comments, "feminist theory in Britain is almost wholly Eurocentric and, when it is not ignoring the experience of black women 'at home', it is trundling 'Third World women' onto the stage only to perform as victims of 'barbarous', 'primitive' practices in 'barbarous', 'primitive' societies".

Black feminist thought emerged as a specific perspective of black women's experiences shaped by both gender and race. Hill-Collins

(1991) argues that black women as a group experience a world different from those who are not black and female. Despite the difference among black women, there is a common thread that binds black women – the struggle against racism and sexism. The experiences of black women include being an outsider within the dominant society and from this position black women have developed specific knowledge and understanding of society. This outsider status gives black women the edge in seeing patterns of belief or behaviour about issues of oppression that may not be available to others. The starting place for this knowledge is lived experiences and a sense of reclaiming the everyday world as self-defined by black women themselves.

Hill-Collins (1991) outlines three dimensions of a black feminist perspective that arise out of shared experiences of being black and female and include long-standing belief systems rooted in an African heritage. First, concrete experience that is described as the combination of knowledge and wisdom derived from lived experiences. Hill-Collins (1991) uses the adage 'who feels it knows it'. This is expressed through African-centred social thought that the lessons of the universe and life are taught through action and motion. This construct understands that people learn lessons of life through living. Second, dialogue as a cultural trait is found in African oral traditions and connects experience with knowledge. This is where black feminists assess knowledge claims; for example, call and response in a group context allows for ideas to be tested. Participation from the group is encouraged so that the speaker is co-active and the power of the word facilitates audience participation. The third element extends to the ethic of caring. Here, emphasis is placed on individual uniqueness as an individual is thought to be a unique expression of a common spirit or energy in life. The ethic of caring involves developing the capacity for empathy and appropriateness of emotions in dialogue. Emotion is expressed through the speaker and indicates that the speaker believes in the argument or discussion. The last element of this perspective relates to the ethic of personal accountability that makes individuals accountable for their values and the consequences of their action.

Brah (2000) outlines a black feminist point of view that addresses issues of difference. She believes it is important to understand the specific histories of racism among black communities because some are reproduced around cultures rooted in a postcolonial experience. Brah (2000) suggests that each ethnic group experiences different patterns of disadvantage and racism and responds in different ways. For example, among Asian groups there are distinctive differences in culture and communities and, in this context, ethnicity and culture should be emphasised rather than race. Brah (2000) points out that difference can be seen through its different meanings. For example, difference can be explained through experience, social relations as subjectivity and identity.

Theories about social change: African-centred social thought

African-centred perspectives have emerged in some black communities as theories of social change. Black studies provides the backdrop for a body of research literature identifying ways of being human and understandings of the world through cultural data in the cultures and philosophies of black people. African-centred worldviews bring together various schools of thought derived from classical African civilisations as the template of cultures, belief systems and values that inform black cultural identities in the modern world. Black communities have taken this knowledge together with life experiences as a framework to bring about social change and empowerment.

Several scholars have applied African-centred perspectives to social work and designed interventions that engage and sustain community building strategies (Schiele, 2000; Graham, 2002, 2005). This framework, known as African-centred social work, seeks to examine the social ills and issues faced by black communities through the lens of black experiences and interpretations. This approach to social work considers oppression to be an important source of problems and difficulties. Schiele (2000) believes that one of the damaging effects of oppression is that it hinders the creation of visions, possibilities and potential in thinking about the future.

Several frameworks of African-centred social work draw on cultural knowledge as a strategy of resistance by interpreting realities outside of Eurocentric lines of social thought, which often locate black people within a consciousness of racism and oppression. These social realities can be empowering because black people frequently have limited choices and opportunities to construct social realities that are meaningful and empowering. Several social action strategies have become established forms of African-centred social work interventions. For example, life cycle development programmes have designed practical ways to support young people into adulthood and family relationships by applying cultural knowledge, themes and patterns.

Theories about black, cultural and minority identities

As many of the histories of black and minority communities are steeped in a colonial past, these experiences frame black identities in Britain. The simplistic understanding of power and discrimination in the opposites of black and white has been replaced by a focus on identities. This shift in thinking was also spurred on by the rise of cultural studies in sociology. Hall (1992) played a leading role in shifting and redefining the idea of race towards ethnicity. The term 'ethnicity' has many meanings and there is no single accepted use of this term. However, ethnicity usually refers to the customs and values associated with groups of people from certain geographical areas. Cultural identity surfaced as a way of understanding groups in a more beneficial way. Hall (1992) was concerned with what it means to be black in British society and how black identities were constructed, claiming that there is no essential black experience but instead diverse social experiences and cultural identities. Cultural identities are not fixed but are continually shifting and there are different forms of racism rather than one form of inequality.

Issues of power

It is important for social workers to appreciate and understand the impact of issues of power, because, as Lymberry and Butler (2004, p 15) maintain, "it is the exercise of power that structures society, shaping the social processes that influence our lives. Power is embedded in political processes as well as personal encounters". Postmodern writing approaches issues of power in a different way than usual thinking on this topic. The postmodern theorist, Foucault, considers that power is more than something that is acquired or possessed in society. The nature of power is spread out and as well as being associated with knowledge it is also connected to the emergence of human service professions and methods of treatment. Methods of treatment are therapies that seek to treat and 'cure' individuals. These treatment approaches involve relations of power that are exercised through social control practices in social institutions. Relations of power are organised in social institutions, and Foucault defines power as a power over others, the power to define others (Sarup, 1988, p 73). In other words, power can be exercised in defining the realities of individuals and social groups through knowledge because certain forms of knowledge have been widely accepted as truth during particular historical periods with the help of various social techniques and procedures.

In the context of social work, professional knowledge can function as an instrument to discipline or control marginalised groups or individuals. This is because professional knowledge can construct what is normal and what is deviant as accepted knowledge to underpin and support institutional practices. These issues have underpinned ongoing discussions about the role and purpose of social work. In exploring the purpose of social work, questions arise about whether the profession is about social reform or changing the system altogether. Should practitioners help clients to 'fit' into society or should social workers be involved in attempting to change the system, or indeed do both? Caring holds a central place in the history and development of social work, and several commentators have highlighted a shift that has taken place in recent years towards activities involving social control. These aspects of control are often exercised in subtle ways and involve availability of resources as well as managing clients and risky behaviour.

White privilege: the invisible knapsack

Over many years, critical race and gender theory has concentrated on bringing to the centre the voices of those historically excluded or on the margins across all disciplines. However, there has been a long silence on questions of whiteness as a social construct. Whiteness carries a positive identity and without racial others it could not exist. It is only recently that white privilege has been discussed both in the US as well as among British authors (Fine et al, 1997; Phoenix, 1997). Some authors have speculated that the reason for the silence surrounding whiteness is because silence about this subject helps to maintain the privileged position of whiteness and obscures the ways in which it is implicated in power relations (McIntosh, 1992; Fine et al, 1997). Fluehr-Lobban (2006, p 168) makes the point that:

> Since being white is the norm, whiteness is invisible to whites. Since whiteness is invisible, the privileges that are conveyed by it are also invisible, unrecognized, and unacknowledged.

In order to understand racism in all its forms, it is essential to include white majority as well as black or minority experiences. Several writers, including Frankenberg (1997), have argued that white majority communities are racialised in such a way that they often accumulate unearned privileges. Frankenberg (1997) goes on to conclude that the act of naming whiteness moves whiteness from its silent and unmarked position that in and of itself is an effect of its dominance.

Although the issues of difference and multiple identities have held a central place in postmodern theories, most social work literature has focused almost exclusively on black identities leaving issues of whiteness unexplored. Understanding how whiteness functions in society has also emerged through a more sophisticated understanding of power relations in society. In order to explain the ways in which the majority society speaks about or represents minorities in various contexts, it is necessary to unpack whiteness as a marker of unearned privilege.

As there has been a tendency to ignore the social construction of whiteness and its connection with racial hierarchy and social divisions, this social knowledge is underdeveloped because for far too long white people have viewed themselves as racially neutral or non-racial. This process assures that the issues of racism are the concern of black and minority people and this focus helps to create an invisible cloak surrounding the advantages of whiteness. Racism involves not only oppression but also privilege and, as Frankenberg (1997) points out, just as men and women's lives are both shaped by their gender, white people and people of colour live racially structured lives.

Peggy McIntosh's (2004, pp 103-8) popular essay entitled 'White privilege: Unpacking the Invisible Knapsack' gives real life examples of the unacknowledged unconscious privilege that the majority population need not be concerned about in their everyday life. Even though McIntosh recognises that hierarchies are interlocking, she believes white privilege is often denied and protected. McIntosh, speaking about her childhood experiences, notes that "I was taught to see racism only in individual acts of meanness, not in invisible systems conferring dominance on my group" and goes on to articulate white privilege in this way:

> I remembered the frequent charges from women of color that white women whom they encounter are oppressive. I began to understand why we are justly seen as oppressive, even when we don't see ourselves that way. I began to count the ways in which I enjoy unearned skin privilege and have been conditioned into oblivion about its existence ... whites are taught to think of their lives as morally neutral, normative and average, and also ideal, so that when we work to benefit others, this is seen as work which will allow 'them' to be more like 'us'.

McIntosh identifies those conditions that attach to skin colour privilege or whiteness rather than class, religion, ethnic status or geographical location although she acknowledges that they are intertwined. McIntosh uses the term 'white privilege' to denote an invisible weightless knapsack of special provisions, maps, passports, codebooks, visas, clothes, tools and blank cheques. Some of these unearned privileges as a white person are identified in the following way:

- I can if I wish arrange to be in the company of people of my race most of the time.
- I can be pretty sure that my neighbours in such a location will be neutral or pleasant to me.
- I can go shopping alone most of the time, pretty well assured that I will not be followed or harassed.
- I can turn on the television or open to the front page of the paper and see people of my race widely and positively represented.
- When I am told about our national heritage or about 'civilisation', I am shown the people of my color made it what it is.
- Whether I use checks, credit cards or cash I can count on my skin colour not to work against the appearance of financial reliability.
- I can remain oblivious of the language and customs of persons of color who constitute the world's majority without feeling in my culture any penalty for such oblivion.
- I can go home from most meetings of organisations I belong to feeling somewhat tied in, rather than isolated, out-of-place, outnumbered, unheard, held at a distance or feared.
- If my day, week or year is going badly, I need not ask of each negative episode or situation whether it has racial overtones.

One of the important aspects of understanding the social construct of whiteness is to uncover the privileges that have remained invisible that equate normality with white culture. This means that there is little or no questioning of the power exercised by dominant groups.

Diversity: the new language of equal opportunity

Since the 1960s, successive governments have introduced legislation to deal with discrimination in recruitment and selection procedures as well as harassment in work organisations. The Race Relations Acts have led the way in providing a framework for action, with the public sector developing equal opportunity policies as the best way forward in addressing inequalities. These policies have been the mainstay in tackling racist practices in recruitment and retention of staff in local authorities and organisations for several decades.

Organisations have been encouraged to become equal opportunity employers driven by concerns about fairness and the need to introduce measures that will avoid or minimise direct discrimination. Equal opportunity policies seek to equalise the starting point by removing barriers at the point of selection. They advocate equality of opportunity for all by not discriminating on the grounds of race, sex, marital status, age, religion, disability and sexual orientation. In other words, UK legislation has tended to favour negative rights, the right not to be discriminated against rather than the positive rights of staff in achieving equality of opportunity in the workplace. Equal opportunity policies are informed by the principle of neutrality and the aim of neutrality is to ensure people are treated in the same way (Robinson, 2006). The goal of 'sameness' ensures that people should be treated equally irrespective of social categories. Robinson (2006) suggests that the sameness approach often leaves organisational structures, values and practices in place and allows the prejudices and stereotypes to go unchallenged, reproducing inequalities, hence the criticism of ineffectiveness.

Although there have been some changes in recruitment procedures that have made a difference to the employment of black and minority people, legislation has failed to significantly improve conditions in the workplace. Bhavnani et al (2005) have reviewed the limited academic and policy-based research about workplace conditions and conclude that racial harassment policies in the workplace are rarely evaluated, and there appears to be no evidence of successful interventions to tackle racism in workplace organisations. This lack of progress of equal opportunity policy initiatives has drawn much criticism from many quarters as black and minority groups continue to be under-represented in many occupations and levels in the private as well as the public sector, despite extensive equal opportunity policy training and active recruitment strategies (Acker, 1992; Kirton and Greene, 2000).

The dissatisfaction with equal opportunity policies has led to the adoption of diversity as an alternative model to deal with issues of discrimination in the recruitment and selection of candidates and in organisations generally. For several years, this management policy has been adopted in the US and Canada as normal business practice. Diversity has become the new language of racial equality and is based on the idea that organisations should recognise differences rather than deny them, moving away from group-based differences towards acknowledging individual differences. This approach seeks to provide an overall strategy that covers many social categories including sex, race, religion, sexual orientation, disability and age.

Much of the frames of reference about diversity are located in the business world that advocates that diversity will make organisations more competitive in the global economy. This line of thinking suggests that through valuing individual differences, and creating conducive environments, for example, team building and mentoring, individuals will be encouraged to work to their full potential in a more creative and productive environment. The main elements of diversity are set out in the following way:

- the valuing, recognising and harnessing of a wide range of individual differences;
- recognition that business advantages do stem from recognising individual differences;
- recognition that there are benefits to be gained in the employment relationship from responding to individual needs (Robinson, 2006).

Diversity as a strategy for equality recognises that everyone has a contribution to make, and emphasises the 'positive' aspects of a diverse workforce rather than previous strategies that concentrated on avoiding or minimising discrimination against various social groups. Diversity management avoids some of the 'backlash' problems associated with equality policies because it is seen as operating in the interests of all employees. In this way, diversity has been designed to be inclusive and a mainstream strategy rather than an add-on activity. The emphasis on the 'positive' features of recruiting a diverse workforce rather than a focus on the 'negative' aspects of organisational culture is a key change in social policy. The 2000 Race Relations (Amendment) Act encapsulates this way of thinking by requiring the public sector to promote race equality. The Act not only deals with direct and indirect discrimination but also regulates local authorities to promote good relations between social groups. Local authorities are required to publish their race equality schemes and to provide evaluation of the effectiveness of their policies.

Many difficulties have surfaced in setting up these schemes and an Audit Commission report in 2003 reported insufficient understanding of race equality in the public sector. Bhavnani et al (2005) refer to reports from the Office of the Deputy Prime Minister (2003), examining the effects of the 2000 Race Relations (Amendment)

Act, which found that local authorities were unsure how to integrate equality and diversity into service delivery and practice.

Another related but different point is that traditional models of equal opportunity tended to separate people by race, ethnicity, age or gender. This means that individuals were separated out and divided rather than seen as a whole person with complex multiple identities shaped by class, race or gender. In the real world, people are subject to the interlocking nature of class, race and gender so that experiences can be gendered and racial or other identities in various contexts and situations. Bhavnani et al (2005, p 72) pointed out that "multiple identities are a lived reality and it is important that people are seen as 'holistic individuals'. They should not be 'objectified' in terms of preconceived political and social categories". Although the introduction of diversity as a main strategy for promoting equality appears to be progressive, several authors have pointed out that issues of racial equality are likely to be submerged or sidelined (Kirton and Greene, 2000; Wrench, 2005).

By exclusively focusing on individual differences, models of diversity tend to avoid group-based disadvantages, and therefore have the potential to neutralise race and gender inequalities through denial of group bias in organisational culture. This means that tensions and conflict in organisations are temporarily absorbed by distinguishing experiences of discrimination as isolated and individual experiences rather than general patterns of inequality, and as such meaningful equality becomes obscured (Robinson, 2006).

Some activists in the field have raised concerns about the spread of diversity management because it appears to be a 'soft' option that avoids attempts to modify the behaviour of managers or employees through training or anti-harassment initiatives. Also diversity strategies tend to dilute or sideline race discrimination by promoting a broader approach. As Wrench (2005, p 74) points out:

> ... this [strategy] does not allow for the fact that some groups have suffered historically from much greater prejudice and exclusion than others. Some groups have been marginalised for generations, with strong and negative social meanings attached to perceived group traits, but this will not necessarily be the same for all those who are considered to fall in the diversity calculus.

Many activists are concerned about the broader approach implicated in the new language of diversity. Unemployment continues to be a major issue in black communities, particularly among young black people. Several research studies have highlighted the problem of racial stereotyping as a feature of some organisational cultures that contributes to the 'glass ceiling effect' with regard to promotion (Bhavnani et al, 2005). Meaningful changes in the recruitment and retention of black employees have been painfully slow, leading to scepticism about organisational policies. Despite the efforts of the Commission for Racial Equality in monitoring and campaigning for equal access and a more conducive work environment, racial harassment continues to be a social problem (Carter et al, 1999). In many organisations, including local authorities, black staff groups have emerged in response to marginalisation and a fear that reporting incidents of racial harassment could lead to reprisals. These staff groups have developed social networks of support and a space where issues can be discussed and action plans developed to promote change in organisations.

Diversity and implications for social care

Social care covers a range of care and protection activities provided by the public sector and social care agencies. In recent years social care has been the subject of many changes in the modernising of social services. National standards and a framework for assessing performance and effectiveness have been introduced to improve the quality of care provided in every sector. These strategies are an important aspect of the government's modernising social services agenda based on a 'what works is what counts' approach to service delivery (DH, 2000). Programmes were set up to improve the organisation, delivery and monitoring of services using targets and performance monitoring to secure better overall services. As the government introduced a managerial and business approach to service provision, there was a shift away from direct welfare provision to the private and voluntary organisations together with a restriction of local expenditure and services.

There has been a long-standing neglect by the public sector in providing appropriate services for black and minority communities. Social policy has encouraged equal access to mainstream services and attempted to remove barriers such as language rather than tackling issues of racism or meeting specific community needs. The Race Equality Unit has published several reports highlighting not only the lack of appropriate services but also a lack of interest in issues of race and ethnicity. It appears that these issues have tended to be sidelined or seen as of little relevance.

Recently, attempts to bring issues of diversity to bear on social care have been adopted as a preferred model for equality of opportunity. By promoting diversity effectively, with its emphasis on inclusion across social categories, it is suggested that social care agencies will be better able to meet the needs of individuals by, for example, extending choice and control. The 2000 Race Relations (Amendment) Act provides a statutory duty to promote race equality and therefore an obligation to deliver appropriate services.

Several research studies asking black and minority communities about access and the services they have received have revealed the sense of frustration of service users about the lack of progress towards equality and the need for action. Taking the views of black service users and communities in mind, Butt et al (2005) have identified barriers to promoting diversity in social care, and these are:

- a lack of knowledge among black and minority ethnic communities of the availability of support;
- a lack of appropriate services;
- poor quality services;
- a lack of choice;
- workers without the skills to communicate effectively;
- workers without the experience and skills needed to work with diverse communities;
- direct and institutional discrimination.

The report then goes on to suggest ways in which organisations can not only stop doing things that create barriers but also consider steps to break down these barriers and successfully promote race equality:

1. Organisations should implement a needs-led approach in policy development and in planning service delivery. This approach will draw on evidence of needs as well as employing workers who have knowledge of the needs of diverse communities. In addition, this approach will engage with service users to make sure their ongoing needs are being met.
2. Organisations should have a policy and monitoring framework to promote diversity. Here organisations are encouraged to have a clear plan about what they are trying to achieve and monitoring strategies to evaluate the delivery of services. This kind of framework is required under the 2000 Race Relations (Amendment) Act and has the potential for establishing a policy and monitoring system.

3. The information collected through monitoring systems can be effectively used by organisations to check on progress in promoting equality and to respond to changing needs.

4. Organisations that include clear plans to promote equality and place a high priority on the development of services for black and minority ethnic communities are more likely to have black and minority ethnic service users. It is apparent that there is a need for both mainstream services and specific services and provision to promote equality.

5. Organisations that engage with black and minority ethnic communities in genuine discussions about priorities and needs are more likely to overcome the lack of knowledge about what support is available.

6. Having a diverse workforce is critical in promoting equality and makes a difference to how organisations engage with diverse communities. It has been suggested that black workers can bring cultural knowledge or competence to service provision although caution needs to be exercised as black workers can be seen as cultural experts, leaving white staff to abdicate responsibility for working with black and minority service users.

Black voluntary organisations have played an important role in establishing services as well as dealing with issues tailored to meet specific needs. Some black and minority service users want services provided by their own community voluntary groups. They feel that mainstream services do not meet the needs of culture, language and beliefs that are important to black and minority communities (Butt and O'Neil, 2004).

Conclusion

This chapter has taken as its starting point the view that oppression operates in different ways to form direct and indirect discrimination. In previous decades, issues of racism and oppression tended to be presented in a broad simplistic way that attracted criticism and denial about everyday realities in British society. Over the years, a rethinking about oppression and social divisions has offered a more complex understanding of social, political, historical and economic factors that have an impact on people's lives. Black perspectives have played an important role in challenging traditional assumptions as well as articulating alternative social realities about life experiences and orientations to knowledge. These ways of thinking have contributed to social work generally and led to culturally specific social work interventions and approaches.

Postmodern outlooks have unlocked the taken-for-granted assumptions that underpin much of social work knowledge and shed light on knowledge as power and its use in professional situations as mechanisms of social control. These theories continue to pose challenges to traditional ways of thinking as well as opening up new areas of everyday life as units of study. Postmodern theories have also shifted thinking about group-based inequalities to more emphasis on individualised understanding of inequality under the umbrella of diversity. These developments tend to dilute and sideline issues of racism both in the workplace and service delivery. Research evidence indicates many black service users do not receive quality services to meet their needs. The shift towards diversity as an integral part of mainstreaming issues of equality may end up pushing these issues off agendas as general patterns of inequality. Instead, these issues will be perceived and dealt with as individual issues rather than as patterns of disadvantage institutionalised within welfare provision.

FOUR

Children and families

Introduction

Social work with children and their families has held a central place in the history and development of professional practice. Social welfare legislation has informed the development of children's services as well as progress made in understanding childhood and the needs of children generally. By tracing the history of child welfare several important changes can be identified. Early child welfare in the Victorian era was characterised by rescuing children through Poor Law actions, but by the early 1900s shifted to the promoting of children's well-being across the fields of education, public health and responsible parenthood. The Child Study movement played a leading role in developing professional knowledge about child development and was highly influential in establishing health, education and welfare services for all children.

Major developments in children's welfare services took place in the 1940s, when the Labour government established comprehensive social welfare institutions to provide state welfare services from the 'cradle to the grave'. The 1948 Children Act provided the legislative framework for the creation of Children's Departments where the particular needs of children and their families became widely accepted among professionals. The Act replaced the Poor Law, with its emphasis on rescuing children, with the promoting of children's welfare and social work practice with the family as a whole. These developments were based on the premise that families have the capacity to care for children, and social workers set about supporting individual families to prevent the admission of children into public care.

Further legislation was introduced in response to public concern about child abuse that highlighted the need for child protection services. Family-based social work focused on intervention and treatment of the family as a dysfunctional grouping. The issues of poverty and disadvantage play an important role in creating many social problems that social workers are faced with in their day-to-day practice – it is widely acknowledged that poverty and social deprivation are closely associated with children suffering severe disadvantages in their lives and being received into public care.

Against this background of policy developments in child welfare and in the context of postwar reconstruction, there was a labour shortage during the 1950s and 1960s. Black people from Commonwealth countries including India, Pakistan, Jamaica and Barbados were actively encouraged to come to Britain to take advantage of jobs in the National Health Service, the textile industry, public transport and catering. In many respects, these sectors of the economy were characterised by low pay and poor working conditions and very few arrangements were made to assist migrants when they arrived in Britain. This lack of assistance was particularly absent in social welfare, where government agencies were of the opinion that migrant workers from the Commonwealth had come of their own volition, therefore no special arrangements should be made to accommodate them. Black people from the Commonwealth countries joined the long-established black communities in various parts of the UK.

On arrival in Britain, black people experienced harrowing levels of racism and discrimination in most areas of social life. Housing was particularly difficult because of widespread discrimination operated by many private landlords. During the 1960s racism was more openly expressed and it was not unusual to see advertisements for rented housing placed by landlords stating 'no coloureds here'.

Black families found it difficult to find suitable accommodation and often had little choice but to accept unsatisfactory rental properties from unscrupulous landlords. As a result of this situation, black families were pushed into already decaying and overcrowded inner cities. Many black families were unable to access local authority housing because they did not meet the eligibility requirements of residency. These housing difficulties came together with widespread discrimination to produce a knock-on effect that exacerbated patterns of social inequality.

Although black people made a substantial contribution to the war effort as well as reconstruction after the war, they were never seen as acceptable as citizens. This point is illustrated by Jacobs (1986, p 13) in the following way:

> ... black workers were acceptable as cleaners, porters, kitchen staff, even nurses and doctors, but never wholeheartedly as patients. They could build council houses but were not expected to live in them.

In the context of widespread racial discrimination, exclusion and social disadvantage, black children were received into the care system at an alarming rate. These factors were also compounded by racism within the social work profession and the ways in which stereotypical ideas about black families had entered social work practice. Community activists, black professionals and others began to draw public attention to the plight of black children in the care system. Several research studies reported on a range of issues surrounding black families and children including evidence that social services failed to adequately meet their needs (Bebbington and Miles, 1989; Rowe et al, 1989; Barn et al, 1997). As these concerns developed, so began the long and sometimes bitter relationship between black communities and social services.

This chapter begins with an overview of key policy issues surrounding the high presence of black children in care and the development of foster and adoption initiatives to address the needs of black children. The next section goes on to look at empowerment and strengths-based models of practice with black families and children. These models of social work practice sought to challenge deficit models of black families that consisted of prevailing myths and stereotypes about lifestyles and to highlight the impact of social disadvantage and discrimination. As the empowerment and strengths models of social work became popular methods across social work practice generally, they dovetailed into legislative requirements to work in partnership with children and their families.

In the following section black children in public care are discussed, including a consideration of the 2000 Children (Leaving Care) Act. The next part of the chapter deals with issues of child protection. Several black children have been the subject of high profile child abuse inquiries, from Jasmine Beckford (Blom-Cooper, 1985), and Tyra Henry (London Borough of Lambeth, 1987) to, more recently, Victoria Climbié in 2003 (Laming, 2003). As a result of the failure of professionals to collaborate in protecting Victoria Climbié, a subsequent public inquiry made a number of recommendations. These recommendations acknowledged that child protection cannot be separated from policies designed to improve children's lives and advocated a framework of integrated children's services. Legislative reforms and new proposals were initiated under the auspices of *Every Child Matters* (DfES, 2004) and the 2004 Children Act to develop children's services and to make visible children who have remained hidden and are most vulnerable to social exclusion.

Background and context: black children in public care

In a landmark study by Rowe and Lambert (1973), they reported on large numbers of children 'drifting' into care without decisions being made to ensure their long-term care. As a result of these findings, this study identified many black children among their sample of children likely to spend their childhood in care. Early perspectives on the placement of black children followed a colour-blind approach that ignored their specific physical, emotional and psychological needs in the context of societal racism and discrimination.

Black children were sometimes placed in residential homes in rural areas away from black communities, cared for by white staff and, as a result, their physical and psychological needs were inadequately considered. These placements were often detrimental to black children because they experienced hurt and rejection when trying to 'fit in' with majority society. Equally important, any links with family members and their communities were severed or difficult to maintain. Through organisations such as Black and In Care, black young people articulated their experiences of racism and inadequate attention to their needs in residential institutions (Black and In Care, 1984).

During the 1970s and 1980s black children in care were often deemed as unlikely to have a family life and seen as 'hard to place' by adoption agencies. Black families were rarely, if at all, considered as foster carers or potential adopters. As the numbers of white babies waiting for adoption decreased, adopters were offered black babies as a last option. During this period it became normal social work practice to place black children with white adopters or foster carers. Many social workers believed that this was a progressive step that supported wider assimilation policies already in place. Following on from this belief, it was argued that black children were better off in trans-racial adoptive placements rather than languishing in residential institutions (Barn et al, 1997). Growing criticism emerged from black communities and professionals about the way social workers dealt with black families and children, and there were calls for changes in social work policy and practice.

Black and anti-racist activists were particularly concerned about black children in public care and the failure of agencies to actively recruit black foster and adoptive carers. This failure to actively recruit black foster and adoptive carers appeared to confirm not only social work's indifference to the needs of black communities but also a way of establishing trans-racial placements as the best parenting experiences for black children. The placement of black children with white families took a political turn and became the centre of heated debates among black communities and wider society. John Small published a series of articles examining the implications for black children and their communities (Small, 1982, 1984). For example, Small (1984) directed attention to the one-way traffic of black children into white families that in part seemed to fulfil wider assimilation policies adopted by most government institutions.

Black professionals and anti-racist social workers challenged policy and practice, advocating for change and an urgent need to move social work policy in a new direction. With this context in mind, the first black agency, New Black Families, was set up in 1980 to recruit black families to adopt and foster black children in the care of Lambeth Social Services. Small writes about this new initiative, explaining that the unit "has brought a new approach to family finding in the sense that its assumptions are very different from more orthodox agencies. It recognises and values the experience and competence of black families as parents and child rearers and accepts the validity of different life styles and child-care practices" (Small, 1982, p 35).

Small maintains that black children should have the opportunity to be placed with families of similar racial and cultural backgrounds. These efforts began to change social work policy and assisted in breaking down the conspiracy of silence that had developed surrounding the high presence of black children drifting through child welfare institutions, often without any long-term plans for their future (Graham, 2002). Many black social work activists striving for change recognised the need for a nationwide organisation to take forward new directions in social work policy with black families to be effective in a wider context. Under the leadership of John Small, Gloria Barnes and David Devine, the Association of Black Social Workers and Allied Professions (ABSWAP) strongly advocated for a legislative framework that addressed race, culture and language in the provision and delivery of services (ABSWAP, 1983). This organisation presented evidence to the House of Commons Select Committee in 1983, and launched a high profile campaign to attract attention to issues concerning black families and welfare institutions. ABSWAP played a major role in shifting social work practice to become more attuned with the needs and aspirations of black children and their families.

Black-led efforts for change in social work also took place in many local authority social services departments where black social workers' groups were set up. A group of London social workers joined forces with local black communities and instigated the 'Soul Kids Campaign' in Lambeth. For the first time there was a coordinated plan to target potential black families to adopt or foster black children.

1989 Children Act

The introduction of the 1989 Children Act (England and Wales) provided a comprehensive legislative framework for children across public and private areas as a result of several child abuse investigations that identified serious gaps in both the law and child protection agencies and the need for major reforms. Key areas of the Children Act are based on the United Nations Convention on the Rights of the Child (UNCRC), where the protection and care of children in family life, education and health was agreed by all but a few countries across the world.

The Children Act is based on the belief that children are best cared for within the family with both parents taking responsibility for and care of the children. The Act also considers that the welfare of the child is paramount when reaching decisions about a child and their upbringing and care. Local authorities are required to safeguard children and promote their welfare. By placing the child at the centre of childcare reform, the Act advanced children's rights by imposing duties on various bodies to have regard to the wishes and feelings of children in a variety of contexts and situations. The term 'looked after children' was also introduced by the Act as a new category that included all children who are either accommodated or 'in care'.

This major piece of legislation makes specific references to children from black and minority ethnic communities, acknowledging their presence, and places a legal requirement to consider a child's racial, cultural, religious and linguistic background in their care and in the provision of services (1989 Children Act, section 22(5)). This provision established the principle that an understanding of a child's background, in particular their ethnicity, must underscore all work with children and is not solely restricted to set-piece decision-making occasions (Barn et al, 1997). O'Hagan (1999) believes that although the 1989 Children Act acknowledges the multicultural nature of British society, on closer inspection the Act uses loophole phrases such as 'give due consideration' and 'have regard to', which can be easily downplayed by local authorities during court proceedings.

The 1989 Children Act uses the wording 'culture' as a statutory requirement in addressing the needs of black and minority children but does not offer guidance about its definition, in particular those aspects of culture that are important in family and childcare social work. Furness (2005) suggests one of the reasons for the absence of a working definition of culture is the danger of perpetuating stereotypes or discrimination based on an assumption of culture as fixed and homogeneous.

As a result of these concerns, childcare social work has tended to avoid discussions about culture and cultural issues as an integral part of anti-discriminatory and anti-oppressive practice. In the absence of a working definition of culture, O'Hagan (1999) suggests that there are indications that the obligations set out in the Act have not been adequately fulfilled. Even though the Children Act has facilitated some positive developments in addressing the needs and care of black children, several research studies report that local authorities have been slow in implementation and overall there are still major gaps in service provision and family support services (Barn, 2001).

Empowerment: an overview

Working in partnership with families and children emerged as a key element of the 1989 Children Act. It was recognised that the professionalism and the expertise of social workers often held patterns of social control over those who used social services. Established social work practices tended to be dominated by a treatment and cure approach. Here, all too often practitioners identified deficits and based interventions solely on problem orientations leaving out a client's strengths or understanding about the situation at hand. Social workers often directed plans of action without active participation of clients. These kinds of approaches were severely criticised by the radical social work movement because they failed to address issues of power between the social worker and client, issues of class and other social constraints initiated through social work practice.

Radical social work was particularly critical of the social control arm of social work and advocated for a more equal role for clients as a consumer of services. The term 'client' was replaced with 'service user'. This shift in language and focus in social work practice also represented changes in political thinking about public services. In this case, a consumer-driven mixed economy of care was introduced, bringing about many changes across social welfare services.

Heffernan (2006, p 140) makes the point that "Managerialism became the ideological force to bring about a transformation in public services. By the early 1990s, the government was talking about service provision in terms of a market economy and, by the late 1990s, the language of market principles or market forces clearly permeated social work theory and practice". To carry out this shift towards a partnership approach in social work practice, the Department of Health published *The challenge of partnership in child protection* practice guide (DH, 1995a), which gives an account of the knowledge, values and skills required for working in partnership with families and children. The main headings in this publication identify the rationale and benefits of adopting this form of social work practice:

- Clients as a source of information: building on knowledge and understanding that service users bring to the working relationship and taking their priorities as the starting point for interventions.
- Citizens' rights: adopting a more open access approach to allow service users to know what is being said about them and opportunities to be involved in decision-making processes that affect their lives.
- Empowering parents: by involving parents and children in decision making this can assist in building self-esteem and confidence, thereby a sense of having some control about their situation and their lives generally.
- Better outcomes: by working in partnership with parents effectiveness was more likely to be achieved through cooperation and working together to achieve goals and objectives (Trevithick, 2005).

Although legislative reforms sought to reframe social work practice with families and children to include models of partnership, empowerment and strengths models started to surface as a way of addressing previous deficit approaches that impacted on black families and children in a detrimental way. Some of these deficit approaches can be traced to underpinning professional knowledge drawn from developmental psychology with its emphasis on an individualised approach to children and their families.

Barbara Solomon's groundbreaking text entitled *Black empowerment* (1976) led the way in introducing empowerment practice as a source of emancipation and critical intervention. Although this text has not been updated it still holds important strategies and themes surrounding oppressed black communities and social work practice. Other key texts followed, bringing feminist approaches to empowerment, and subsequently notions of empowerment entered social work generally as a core theme to be applied across all areas of social work activity (Braye and Preston-Shoot, 1995; Gutierrez et al, 1998; Adams, 2003).

In the first place, the notion of empowerment was closely associated with social movements as a way of gaining collective political power as well as transforming individuals and increasing their capacity to gain power over their own lives. Black empowerment builds on the civil rights movement that sees empowerment as liberation from oppressive barriers and a sense of rising up and changing one's situation. The phrase 'the personal is political' encapsulates this idea. Empowerment in social work practice has certainly had an impact on social work processes. This empowerment orientation, with its focus on collaboration and competence, contrasts with a tendency to focus on deficits and dysfunction in families. However, there are two angles in empowerment practice that have produced tensions and critical discussions about the meaning of empowerment and its misuse as a wholly positive requisite for practice. Payne (2005, p 302) notes some of the concerns in adopting empowerment practice:

> The use of empowerment as a fashionable concept creates an idealistic and perhaps misleading objective for practice in a period when the role of social work agencies is increasingly limited to protection or service provision. Equally, it may be used as an objective because providing comprehensive services is difficult in a restricted financial environment. This is a misuse of the term, since the assumption of empowerment practice is that workers lend their power to a client for a period to assist them to take power permanently through helping them attain control over their lives. Workers need resources to do this. Moreover, we should not mistake empowerment for enablement.

One of the potential difficulties with the notion of empowerment is that it is often perceived by social work as solely an individual means of breaking down barriers to achieve social objectives and contribute to social change. This approach assumes that people will be able to experience empowerment without having access to resources or with limited options. Empowerment not only hinges on having opportunities and choices on an individual level but is interrelated across personal, interpersonal and political-structural levels. Social workers applied empowerment-oriented practice by working in collaboration with clients and viewing clients as capable and having strengths. This approach strives to engage clients in their own empowerment to align both personal and political resources.

In the political arena recently, empowerment is often embraced through this individualised understanding as a way of avoiding addressing patterns of structural inequalities. But other commentators point to the positive aspects of empowerment practice because it facilitates collaborative and partnership approaches (DuBois and Miley, 2002).

Elsewhere, Graham (2004) believes professional definitions of empowerment tend to neglect black communities' own interpretations, experiences and cultures as a source of ideas and new perspectives. For many black communities, empowerment has its origins in collective struggles when black organisations and individuals sought to address the impact of deep-seated racism and discrimination in British society. The need for empowerment is rooted in the context of racism and discrimination. Empowerment is an essential part of collective struggles because it is often experienced through affirming identities and the process of resistance to external forces. Community activism has provided assistance in dealing with education, employment issues and concerns about negative policing policies and the law. These social action strategies created new ideas and visions for better futures as communities search for ways forward.

This is the starting point for Solomon (1976) as she articulates the ways in which black people are marginalised individually and collectively and, in a social work context, applies the notion of empowerment to bridge the gap between individuals and society. Solomon emphasises empowerment as a process and goal for oppressed people. By infusing empowerment practice, social work has the potential to be emancipatory and to work towards social transformation. Solomon's model of social work helped to shift practice away from psychodynamic themes with their emphasis on blaming the victim to taking into account complex social structures that often generate social problems.

According to Solomon (1976) black communities experience both direct and indirect power blocks operating both separately and together to oppress the communities and to generate powerlessness in various ways. Direct power blocks are located in social institutions that operate mechanisms of discrimination. This kind of discrimination is institutional and operates through day-to-day activities. Indirect power blocks bring the impact of discrimination to the personal realm where negative valuations from the wider society can become incorporated into family processes and restrict the development of personal resources (Graham, 2002).

Even though social work has gained a more sophisticated understanding of power, Solomon's work articulates the experiences of belonging to a stigmatised group and incorporates the histories and unique set of experiences of black families as an influential part of social work interventions. In social work practice, this is 'starting with the client' and involving them in designing social work interventions.

Dalrymple and Burke (1995) outline various levels of the empowerment process from the personal to the political and in so doing they use an empowerment perspective to help clients increase their comprehension of social and political realities. Clients are encouraged to tell their stories and to reflect on various life situations and events to raise self-consciousness and develop a stronger sense of self. In this process, personal biography is taken seriously and dialogue promoted as a way of moving towards critical consciousness. Dalrymple and Burke (1995) suggest that this process can be an empowering experience.

Social workers practising from this perspective recognise and acknowledge black people's daily life experiences in the context of societal racism. Practitioners are sensitive to the social realities of black people's lives and acknowledge the impact of racism on psychological well-being. The social worker collaborates with the client to identify their strengths and the strengths that may be found within the immediate family, friends and community. These factors are important to limit feelings of isolation and the role of the social worker is to identify strengths and support systems and maximise their usefulness for the benefit of the client. In this way, social work is part of the support system as well as a resource and advocate in dealing with life difficulties. In applying these frameworks of empowerment to everyday practice there are assumptions that underlie the process of empowerment (Manning et al, 2004).

Empowerment-oriented practice

- Empowerment is a process that involves clients and practitioners working together as partners.
- Empowerment-oriented practice views clients as having competence and capabilities when given access to resources.
- Clients are encouraged to perceive themselves as causal agents and able to effect change.
- Competence is acquired through life experiences. Black people's narratives of struggles in hostile environments are affirmed as strengths and competence.
- There are many factors involved in any given situation and this requires a diverse approach in seeking solutions.
- Informal networks are an important source of support in stressful situations and in increasing one's sense of control.
- People must be allowed to define their own empowerment rather than have a version of empowerment imposed on them.
- Empowerment involves access to resources and the capacity to use those resources effectively.

> • Empowerment requires a level of awareness and information for change to occur.
> • Empowering practice is dynamic and evolutionary and calls for non-traditional approaches that engage families and communities.
> • Empowerment can be achieved across individual, organisational, political, sociocultural and economical levels.
>
> *Source:* Adapted from DuBois and Miley (2002)

Strengths of black families

Empowerment models in social work are closely associated with strengths-based approaches that have developed into widely accepted forms of practice. A strengths perspective serves as the basis for empowerment because this form of practice looks at strengths as the starting point for working in collaboration with clients. Many perspectives about black families focus on their strengths, in part as a response to the negative representations of black families held by many social workers and the social science literature generally. Strengths refer to culturally based beliefs and values that enable families to meet the needs of their members. Although these attributes and cultural patterns are not exclusive to black families and are found among other minority groups, they contribute to the resilience of black families in dealing with the demands made on families from outside forces (Belgrave and Allison, 2005).

At first, in identifying the strengths of black families in Britain, black authors used African American literature because this content seemed to address many similarities. In the British context, identifying strengths helped to counter negative representations about black families in social work that fostered a devaluation of care giving and child rearing practices in black communities. According to Bernard (2001), the negative representations of black families influenced judgements of what constitutes good enough parenting in black families. Bernard (2001, p 14) then goes on to point out the effects of applying the yardstick of white middle-class norms as a standard to judge black families:

> By implicitly using the experiences of white nuclear middle-class families as normative, the state reinforces a particular image of white middle-class motherhood against which all mothers are judged, and in the process has pathologised black motherhood as deficient. Assumptions about good

enough mothering make more likely, it could be argued, that if you are a black and working class mother, you will be more liable to be a target for state surveillance. Thus, it is suggested that black people may not necessarily see professional helpers as protectors of their communities, but may indeed see them as reinforcing oppression.

By advocating the strengths of black families, the histories of struggles and indicators of resilience are recognised and acknowledged. In this way, knowledge about black families is placed within the broader context of racism in the wider society. In the absence of knowledge about black families in many social work texts, their positive attributes and family patterns need to be included to assist practitioners to make more accurate assessments about problems and difficulties in black families as well as promoting family preservation and cohesion.

Although it is claimed that these strengths are important for the survival, stability and advancement of black families, over time the strengths of black families have become less acceptable in social work because they tended to gloss over or obscure the issues of gender and unequal power relations as well as child maltreatment in black families (Bernard, 2002). Instead, 'strengths' have been redefined as general characteristics, resiliency factors or resources found in many black families. These resources still have a place in the broader aspects of black experiences and perspectives and can form part of a wider context of assessment and social work activities.

While discussion about the strengths of black families has been useful in generating a more considered understanding of black families generally, the background of colonialism as a key factor in understanding the experiences and perspectives of black communities has received little attention. The histories of colonial rule play an important role in understanding social relations between black communities and British society. As Blakemore and Boneham (1994, p 33) observe, "Black and Asian migrants to Britain came from societies which had been deeply affected by white colonialism. In the case of slavery in the Caribbean, this again included attempts to eradicate ethnic identities by suppression of African languages and cultures. British colonialisation of the Indian subcontinent took a different form and relied mainly on 'indirect rule' through Indian states".

Colonialism played an important role in reinforcing racist ideas through cultural superiority and this form of oppression was played out in the themes and propaganda of the British Empire. The legacy of colonial rule and its residual elements add another layer and dimension to black experiences in present-day society. Fanon (1967) explored the process of colonialism and its effects on colonised peoples and, in particular, black people of African descent. He looked at the demeaning representations of blackness and exposed the deep psychological effects of colonialism on both the victims and the colonisers. Black people are defined by the white world under the 'white gaze' and are denied humanity and subject to racial stereotypes. These experiences draw attention to the capacity of society to undermine a person's mental health through a calculated disrespect for difference "so a person or group of people can suffer real damage, real distortion, if the people or society around them mirror back to them a confining or demeaning or contemptible picture of themselves" (Taylor, 1994, pp 25-6).

For many black people experiences of disrespect can become a source of motivation for acts of resistance articulated through black civil rights and anti-colonial social movements. The experiences of disrespect are associated with experiences of non-recognition and the marker of exclusion that can inflict significant harm from low self-esteem to self-depreciation as a potent instrument of oppression. The act of identifying the strengths of black families also became important in establishing black communities' sense of integrity and parental competence in caring for children.

Strengths of black families

1. The survival of black families in the context of enslavement, colonialism and oppression that have sought to destroy black family life.

2. Spirituality is a common cultural value framing the worldviews and lives of black people throughout the world. There is an acceptance of a non-material higher force present in all life's affairs. Expression of spirituality has often take place in religious organisations and churches and these social practices have been identified as key factors in sustaining families and promoting resilience.

3. Black families place great value on education and knowledge as a way of counteracting the effects of oppression and discrimination. The desire for education is expressed in the long-standing institutions of Saturday schools located in black communities.

4. Kinship bonds are an important aspect of black families. A definition of family includes members who are not biologically related, including an extensive network of cousins. The idea of illegitimacy is generally unknown, so all children are seen as legitimate. Black families have traditionally adopted children informally and these children retain their names as an important link to their lineage and kinship to their biological parents.

5. Community self-help continues to be an important aspect of black family life. Self-help is built on notions of exchange and reciprocity that are active social patterns in many communities.
6. The adaptability of family roles among some black families. This approach to family life includes flexibility in sharing caring responsibilities to meet the needs of children and the family generally. The positive attempts of black fathers to rear their children have received little attention generally and instead the deviant behaviour of black men is a widely held perception in the wider society.

Source: Adapted from Graham (2002)

Black children in care

Even though there has been a high presence of black children in care since the 1960s and 1970s, there have been few research studies documenting their experiences in care or recognition of their particular needs and concerns. Black children and their experiences of public care and other social institutions in society are largely hidden on the outer edges of research agendas. It is often assumed that a 'one size fits all' approach will somehow 'naturally' include black children and bring particular issues and concerns into view. This situation is a familiar pattern of oppression whereby the marginal status of black children remains hidden and is maintained by colour-blind approaches in social work. As a result of this process, black children experience a paradoxical oppression in that they are both marked out by stereotypes in the wider society and yet at the same time are made invisible.

Children who come into care are already at a disadvantage and in most cases their life chances have been limited by factors outside their control. For black children, these factors are compounded because they live in societies where their personhood is often devalued or they receive little acknowledgement of their competence and abilities to narrate their lived experiences (Graham, 2006a). Thomas (2005) acknowledges the need for social workers to understand the different patterns of disadvantage and the ways in which young people may be discriminated against not only in the wider society but also by the very services that have been set up to help them.

The high presence of black children in care also includes children of dual heritage and the term 'mixed parentage' is often used to describe this group of children. There has been a growing body of literature looking at issues of identity and disadvantage that impact on their admission into care. Goldstein (1999) provides a review of research from a historical starting point about black children of dual heritage with particular emphasis on the complexities surrounding identities and implications for social work. Although identity issues are dealt with briefly in this chapter, there is not enough space to attend to the full range of controversial issues and complexities surrounding children of dual heritage. However, suffice to say, black children of dual heritage are a significant group who require more attention to be given to understanding their lived experiences and developing professional knowledge to support their particular needs and aspirations.

Before reviewing some of the current legislation about leaving care and young black people, the chapter looks at some of the policy issues in connection with the quality of care and concerns about black identities. As well as trans-racial placements, the quality of care of black children in residential homes provoked critiques from various quarters, perhaps mostly strongly from black professionals. These issues varied from physical care, including hair and skin care, to psychological and emotional well-being, with a tendency to focus on identity and self-esteem. As many black children were placed away from black communities in rural settings, their physical needs were often neglected or inadequately addressed.

One of the areas of concern was hair care and a tendency to cut black children's hair as a way of managing it rather than becoming informed about black hair care and maintenance. The consequences of this lack of care meant that black children sometimes appeared unkempt and black people in various communities often remarked that they could tell if a black child was in care by their appearance. In a similar way, there was concern about skin care that tended to attract attention to the overall care of black children.

As the high presence of black children in care became known, issues surrounding their identity began to surface to become the single most important issue in social work. Many black professionals and others argued that a positive black identity was crucial to the well-being of black children away from their families. They argued that the development of a positive black identity cannot be left to chance because of the depth of racism and socialising influences in British society that were antagonistic to the formation of black identities. This meant that black children away from their families were particularly vulnerable because black families transmit survival mechanisms and can act as a buffer away from the harsh realities of social life (Small, 1984; Maxime, 1987).

Issues surrounding identity and cultural heritage in the care of black children developed into the cornerstone of arguments against trans-racial adoptions. Banks (1999b, p 18) defines a positive black identity as being "one where children have an unmistakable confidence and belief in self and own ethnic group worth, without being dismissive of other cultural or ethnic groups, and are able to accept and feel good about their own culture and 'colour' without denigrating other groups".

There are different perspectives on black identity development and perhaps the best known model is Cross (1978, 1980), where the process of developing a black identity is presented in stages that move from pre-encounter where a black person accepts a white frame of reference to a final stage of internalisation when he or she achieves an inner security and self-confidence with his or her blackness. Robinson (2000, p 6) explains the stages of development:

> In the pre-encounter stage the person is likely to view the world from a white frame of reference [eurocentric].... In the second stage, 'encounter', some shocking or social event makes the person receptive to new views of being black and of the world. The person's eurocentric thinking is upset by an encounter with racial prejudice which precipitates an intense search for black identity.... The third stage, that of immersion–emersion, is the period of transition in which the person struggles to destroy all vestiges of the 'old' perspective.... In the final stage, internalisation, the person focuses on things other than him or herself and his or her ethnic or racial group.

Even though this model applies to black people, similar processes have been proposed for other minority groups (see Kim, 1981).

Although it was recognised that many children from various backgrounds would benefit from identity work, developing a black identity became the concentrated focus for black children. Owusu-Bempah (1997) is critical of this development because social work has been overly influenced by assumptions about black people's identity issues at the expense of wider structural factors deeply rooted in social institutions that create inequalities in resources and opportunities for black children generally. He suggests that the focus on the 'problems' of black identities have a tendency to promote representations of pathology and deficits. Notwithstanding these important critiques developments in direct work with black children has uncovered the identity needs of children generally and the importance of culturally holding environments.

Black children leaving care

While the 1989 Children Act required local authorities to support young people leaving care, the Act imposed few direct responsibilities. The links between the leaving care experience, homelessness, unemployment, social isolation and the lack of educational qualifications is significant. The government's Social Exclusion Unit reported in 1998 that "between a quarter and a third of rough sleepers have been looked after by local authorities as children" (1998, p 5). Several studies identified serious gaps in planning and the provision of services, and also reported on poor outcomes for young people leaving care even though there had been some gradual improvement overall (Biehal et al, 1995; Barn et al, 2005).

Against the background of inconsistencies in the provision of services, young people leaving care face continuing problems through the transition to adulthood and independence (Stein, 1997; Broad, 2005). Young people have been expected to leave care and be independent at an earlier age than the majority of young people in the general population so there was an expectation of becoming 'independent' between the ages of 16 and 18. This expectation goes against national trends that point to a longer transition into adulthood in most family situations.

Being independent at such a young age placed on young people leaving care responsibilities of adulthood that they were ill equipped and prepared for. Many young people leaving care found themselves faced with how to manage a home, start a career and manage close relationships without preparation and with few or no support systems or informal networks. The lack of personal and emotional support can be devastating for young people. Teenage pregnancy is high among this group of young people and often follows shortly after leaving care. As many young people are ill prepared for leaving care, it is not surprising that they often experience considerable difficulties in living, including a high risk of homelessness. These factors paint a bleak picture of care leavers particularly as these young people came into the care system in the first place because of multiple difficulties and disadvantages in their families. The over-representation of black children in public care means that young black people are disproportionately represented as a group of care leavers.

While a body of literature has raised awareness about the problems facing young people leaving care, there is a lack of research and knowledge about the specific needs and concerns of young black people leaving care (Graham, 2006a). There is anecdotal evidence that young black people experience racism in care as well as in the wider society. They felt that the lack of cultural knowledge affected their confidence and self-esteem. Black and In Care, an organisation formed to give voice to young black people in the care system, identified the following issues at a conference in 1984:

- residential units employed mainly white staff;
- there was a lack of black staff in management positions;
- there was both overt and covert racism in the care system;
- the effects of loss of racial identity remained with young black people into their adulthood (Ince, 2004).

These concerns voiced by young black people were echoed in a study by the national organisation for young people leaving care, First Key, in 1987. This study reported on the provision of services in three London boroughs and young black people's experiences of the care system and leaving care. Although these studies raised the profile of the difficulties of young black people, there was very little impact on care services overall. In a more recent study by Ince (1998), young black people voiced their care experiences and what happened to them after they left care institutions. One of the important issues highlighted in this study is the consequences of disengagement of young black people from their families and communities. Ince (1999, p 160) points out that:

> ... prolonged and extensive periods in care exposed all of the young people to a white Eurocentric model of care, with adverse implications for reintegration with their family and community. This was a key variable in their perceptions of themselves and their ability to cope after leaving care. Restricted contact with parents, relatives, black friends and the wider black community diminished the extent to which opportunities were presented for cultural exchange and conscious awareness of being black. The role of the black family in acting as a buffer and offering protection for the child from a hostile society is an extremely important one for black children living in Britain.

While the 1989 Children Act promotes children's right to a voice and opportunities to participate in decisions that affect their lives, black children's voices are rarely heard. Bearing this in mind, Ince's small-scale study has particular significance in opening up spaces for black children to give voice to their experiences and concerns, as well as drawing attention to the specific needs of young black people leaving care. Ince (1999) concludes that a process of identity stripping is experienced by many young black people in care institutions and emphasises that, without a positive sense of identity, these young people have difficulty in making the transition into adulthood successfully.

In another study, entitled *The care experience:Through black eyes* (NCB, 2004), young black people speak about the importance of education as being critical to their life chances.They felt that the educational system often stigmatised young black people as trouble makers, and teachers perceived them as underachievers.This situation was particularly acute for young black people in care because poor levels of educational attainment and high levels of unemployment and poverty are factors that featured more frequently in their lives.These young people wanted to have love and security and to be cared for and accepted for who they are and helped through their difficulties, retaining links with relatives and communities. In addition, they felt that sometimes social workers did not recognise that they have a history, a people and origins that extend beyond the UK and Europe, and social realities as young black people growing up in modern-day Britain (NCB, 2004).

2000 Children (Leaving Care) Act

The 2000 Children (Leaving Care) Act (England and Wales) was introduced alongside Quality Protects initiatives to improve the quality of state childcare. Goddard (2003) explains that the development of the Act rests on three factors. First, a body of research reported on past and current inadequacies of leaving care policy and practice. Second, there was official recognition of the failure to produce good outcomes for children in state care, and, third, the Labour government developed a strong commitment to tackle social exclusion.

The Act provides a framework for leaving care services and local authorities remain responsible for the welfare of care leavers between the ages of 18 and 21. It introduces new guidance and regulations including pathway planning to help care leavers to move through the process of independent living in a longer time frame so that they have opportunities to gain basic life skills and are more prepared generally for adulthood. This means every young care leaver should receive a comprehensive plan with a clear route to independence. Goddard (2003, p 27) explains that "this assessment was designed to aid the leaving care planning process. It determines the form and levels of advice, assistance that support young people require – both while they remain looked after and afterwards – and forms the basis of a 'Pathway Plan' for the transition to independence".

Barn et al (2005) maintain that pathway planning should give attention to a young person's capacity to manage independently and advocate for leaving care services to invest more time and resources in skill-building programmes. For young people who are undertaking further education and training, the provision of support lasts beyond the age of 21, and with increased concern about improving the quality of education for care leavers these new initiatives will be particularly important. Personal advisers are available for care leavers to implement pathway plans that take account of the young people's own wishes and preferences. The personal adviser provides advice and support as well as coordinating services and keeping in touch with the young person.

Other measures, such as the appointment of designated teachers, have been introduced to raise the priority of education to improve educational achievement and support. Although these new developments have been welcomed, it remains to be seen whether the Act will prove to be a successful long-term solution to some of the problems of care leavers. Because these changes are long overdue further steps may be required to improve the life chances of care leavers. These long-term aims are initiated to ensure that care leavers do not have to start their adult life with multiple disadvantages and that they receive the kind of care and support they need and deserve.

Child abuse and neglect

Concerns about child abuse and neglect can be traced to the end of the 19th century when social reformers set up voluntary organisations to deal with child cruelty and the well-being of children. Following these early perspectives, working with children and families has become one of the most important areas of social work. Over time child abuse has received a great deal of public attention as a result of child deaths, and followed a pattern of being 'discovered' and then ignored. For example, the 'discovery' of child abuse was linked to the battered child syndrome in the 1960s and sexual abuse both within and outside the family in the 1970s and 1980s. These patterns of concern in child abuse, and, more recently, child protection, have shifted from a narrow focus on child neglect and physical abuse to increased awareness of different forms of abuse and maltreatment, including emotional abuse. With the increased knowledge and awareness of child abuse, this area of practice has become one of the most controversial and stressful areas of social work practice.

One major landmark in child welfare was the inquiry into the death of Maria Colwell in 1974 that proved crucial in establishing child abuse as a major social problem and in introducing fundamental changes in policy and practice (Parton, 1985). The public inquiry into this tragic death of a child attracted widespread media attention and influenced public attitudes to social work. Social workers were heavily criticised and seen as failing to protect children, sometimes as a result of professional incompetence. These failures in the child protection system have placed the safety of children under intense public scrutiny with demands for more accountability and professional training for social workers. While there have been more than fifty public inquiries since 1974 into child abuse cases, the lack of coordination and the breakdown in communication between professionals in the child protection system continues to be a major contributory factor in failing to protect children.

Most public inquiries have brought about new legislation and regulations resulting in initiatives to prevent child abuse and new frameworks for detecting and monitoring families at risk. These developments happened against the background of the changing landscape of social work and social care generally. Cuts in public expenditure as well as inadequate resources to meet the demands of child protection services have all taken their toll on social services. Added to these difficulties, social workers often experience stress and sometimes hostile organisational arrangements that surround the practice of social work in state institutions. Various changes in social policy have brought about privatisation of social services, consumer-driven initiatives and the introduction of managerialism in social services organisations leading to a remaking of social work with children with families.

The high profile cases of Jasmine Beckford, and subsequent inquiry report in 1985, and then Tyra Henry in 1987 brought into sharp focus issues of child protection in black communities (Blom-Cooper, 1985; London Borough of Lambeth, 1987). How has social work responded to black families and issues of child abuse and neglect? First of all, Chand (2000) points to the little attention given to these issues in British social work research and literature although black families are present in child protection caseloads. Other available research presents a confusing picture and part of the problem here seems to be the diverse nature of black communities with a wide range of social, economic and cultural expectations between groups. This lack of attention to child protection issues and black communities extends to the Department of Health's important publication, *Child protection: Messages from research*

(DH, 1995b). This report was clearly a missed opportunity to include black families in research agendas and subsequent training activities in social services departments throughout Britain.

As a result of this gap in the research literature there is a lack of professional knowledge about patterns of family life in black communities and the impact of discrimination and social inequalities generally. One of the reasons given for the absence of this literature is the lack of ethnicity data available from social services departments, since ethnic monitoring was only recently introduced. However, this explanation seems inadequate given concerns over the limited skills of social services staff when undertaking assessments and designing interventions with black families (Williams and Soydan, 2005).

Chand (2000) suggests that there are two underlying contexts that frame understanding of black families in child abuse investigations. The first approach is the pathologising of black families that "incorporates the view that black people, their cultures and lifestyles are inherently problematic and need correcting" (Singh, 1992, p 19). In this case, social workers utilise cultural deficit models of black families and may intervene unnecessarily or over-rely on cultural explanations of child abuse. In this context, black families are often subject to higher levels of surveillance or receive more punitive interventions when compared to the majority population, particularly when families are disadvantaged.

The second approach is cultural relativism that means "that all cultures are equally valid in formulating human relationships. Thus members of one culture have no right to criticise members of another culture by using their own standards of judgment" (Channer and Parton, 1990, p 111). This approach, together with the 'rule of optimism', seems to operate with black families, whereby the most favourable interpretation is always put on the behaviour of the parents. This is because 'natural love' will overrule all other considerations and that anything that may question this ideal is discounted. As a result of these approaches and fears of accusations of racism, many social workers hesitated to intervene appropriately with black families. This point is considered by Brophy (2003, p 674): "Balancing a respect for differing styles of parenting and guarding against inappropriate inroads into lifestyles and belief systems, while also protecting children from ill-treatment, remains an exacting task. Professionals can be castigated for using statutory interventions too quickly, or too slowly (as in the case of Victoria Climbié)". Clearly, there are other issues that come into play in the child protection system, including language difficulties, poverty, unemployment, assessment processes and discrimination within social work institutions.

One particular area of concern in social work studies is the use of interpreters in cases where families speak little or no English (Chand, 2005). This language barrier can place black and Asian families at great disadvantage in the assessment process. Chand (2000, p 71) highlights some of difficulties in using an interpreter because many social workers believe that "every bilingual individual is suitable and competent to interpret all situations, but this is not the case; the concepts associated with child abuse and neglect are very different from those concerning, for example, welfare rights".

Using interpreters brings some complex issues including ensuring that interpreters are available and that they can accurately and sensitively communicate with the families that they are serving. To ensure a beneficial outcome, this process will need to be carefully planned with arrangements that often require more time. Humphreys et al (1999, p 285) make the point that:

> ... understanding clearly what is happening at every step along the way is an essential element in making sure that this difficult process is not exacerbated by communication problems between professionals and the family. This problem is not unique to those who are not fluent in English. The misunderstandings, poor communication and mystification of professional language and processes have been a source of complaint by many families who become caught up in the child protection system.

However, Humphreys et al (1999) also point out that even though child protection is an essential service, interpreting services receive little attention in the research literature or training and this gap helps to perpetuate a Eurocentric approach to work with black children and their families.

Although Chand (2005) acknowledges that some interpreting services in child protection provide an excellent service, there are others that need to improve standards. These improvements include better-trained interpreters who are knowledgeable of child protection generally, and more training for social workers to work more effectively with interpreters. Social workers need to recognise that language is more than just a way to communicate – it holds important cultural ties and a sense of belonging and identity.

The 1989 Children Act acknowledges the importance of support services for children and families in need. It provides accompanying guidance that services will be provided in partnership with children and families. Ahmed (2005), in a review of preventative services for black families, reports that there is limited evaluated evidence of family support services for black families that may reflect an overall lack of services. The level of family support services for black families in need is a key factor in curbing the pattern of rapid entry of black children into public care. Indeed, Barn (1993) has consistently maintained that it is a core dimension of institutional racism that there is a lack of relevant services because they play an important role in preventing the over-representation of black children in public care.

Williams and Soydan (2005) note that there are dangers in imposing both Eurocentric practice and overly cultural relativist practice. Eurocentric practice imposes a set of cultural beliefs as universal and usually reproduces patterns of domination. On the other hand, by imposing extreme cultural relativism, judgements about care can be used to justify a lesser standard of care for some children. The problem is finding a balance between these concerns as social work operates mainly through a colour-blind approach with a universal formula and standards of good practice that can be established and that fit all. On a broader scale, by leaning on universal approaches, social work is endorsing the view that black families should assimilate through liberal notions of equality while offering simple solutions to complex life issues. Williams and Soydan (2005, p 903) draw out the implications for social workers:

> Practitioners may, therefore, retreat into colour-blindness out of fear or lack of confidence. The justification frequently offered for this approach is that ethnic minority clients are adequately served within mainstream institutional interventions and to demarcate specialist provision is unnecessary, ineffective and may even do them a disservice. This laissez-faire approach is widely regarded to have failed ethnic minorities.

Giving voice to black children

Since the introduction of the 1989 Children Act there has been a general movement towards children's rights and opportunities for them to have a greater say in the decisions that affect their lives. These trends build on the UNCRC, which outlines a new vision of the child as an individual and as a member of a family and community with rights and responsibilities appropriate for her or his age. Alongside these developments, sociologists have employed 'new' ways of thinking about children and childhood in modern society. Children are viewed as active participants whose actions can both change and shape their daily lives in various contexts and situations. From this perspective, the social context of children's lives is emphasised as they are given agency as social people in the fullest sense.

Several writers consider that in this context we know very little about children's ordinary lives and their own interpretations and experiences (Christensen and Prout, 2005). The nature of childhood has also been subject to a rethinking and recognition that there are diverse childhoods that are linked to social positions and status in society. This attention to the social experiences of children and the broader contexts of their lives brings issues of race, gender and disability to the table and offers a more inclusive picture of childhood. This frame of reference has particular relevance for black children because they live in societies where their personhood is often devalued or they receive little acknowledgement of their competence and abilities to narrate their lived experiences (Graham and Bruce, 2006).

On a related but different point, giving voice to experiences has long been a call by black people in defining their own experiences and presence in knowledge of social life. This lack of voice has been extended to black children who often have few opportunities in which their voices can be heard and in particular their lived experiences in social institutions such as families, schools or in public care (Graham, 2006a).

While issues of gender have been explored in Childhood Studies, less attention has been paid to issues of social difference and the ways in which black children experience childhood taking into account the broader context of society. A growing body of literature has looked at new ways of thinking about childhood and a focus on children's perspectives has led to the adoption of a 'social child' perspective for social work that actively engages children's participation and their lived experiences in social institutions, including public care (Thomas, 2000; Thomas and O'Kane, 2000). This growing recognition of children's perspectives on the social world has applications for direct work with children.

Thomas and O'Kane (2000, p 830) suggest established models of practice can be expanded or reframed to integrate participatory approaches to harness "a wealth of experience in dealing with children on their own terms and helping them to make sense of their lives". The everyday lives of children hold important information about children's relationships with social workers and child welfare institutions. Social work often deals with children in difficult situations and circumstances away from their families and environments yet we know very little about children's own interpretations or understanding of these experiences. What are the perceptions and views of children when they are involved with welfare institutions? What participatory opportunities are available for children to talk about experiences, social achievements and competences that translate into new avenues of practice?

For children in public care, Sandbaek (1999) proposes that there is a pressing need to shift dominant ways of thinking about children receiving services as 'problems' to viewing them as competent witnesses to their lives. Sandbaek's (1999) innovative study sets out to reframe the view of children with 'problems', which she believes is biased because this frame of reference does not include knowledge from children themselves. This deeper understanding of children's interests, successes and important people in their lives can enhance practice by perceiving children as active agents and giving voice to their views and perceptions about the welfare services they receive. Professional knowledge about children in public care largely stems from developmental models that tend to focus on pathology and specifically 'problem' children. This can be particularly detrimental for children from socially stigmatised groups who are subject to majority representations and stereotypes in the wider society.

The recognition of social achievements that children themselves regard as successes and positive experiences can enhance opportunities to give voice to their views and perceptions about the welfare services they receive. The focus on these protective factors can assist children in stressful circumstances where they often struggle to find opportunities to develop competence and confidence. By opening spaces and giving voice to their experiences, new possibilities can come to light through building on children's positive experiences and areas of competence. These opportunities also open up attention to giving voice to lived experiences of difference and speaking about everyday racisms from the vantage point of children themselves. By employing these strategies, children can be empowered to have their own accounts of their lives and appropriate consideration of their wishes and feelings taken seriously.

Social model of childhood: implications for child welfare

- Children's everyday lives and experiences help shift professional knowledge from the usual description of children with 'problems' to a deeper understanding of children.
- Their interests.
- Their successes.
- People who are important in their lives.

Graham and Bruce (2006) have extended the 'social child' perspective currently applied to social work and proposed an approach to practice with black children that considers the lived experiences of black children as well as encouraging them 'to have a say' through active participation in decision-making activities. Graham and Bruce (2006) suggest that integrating the lived experiences of black children from their vantage point in decision making can help to shift emphasis away from deficit models of 'problem' children to a deeper understanding of social achievements and competences of black children. This approach can strengthen positive elements of their lives as well as help raise self-esteem.

Equally important, by allowing black children to take part in their own care and ensuring they have time to properly understand the issues, in the longer term there would be a qualitative difference in children's experiences of public care. Black children are less likely to feel alienated from decision-making processes and instead have a sense of active participation in decisions made about their lives. Another point is that the participation of children in decision-making activities has the potential to accord children both recognition and protection. For children who have been abused or neglected, this approach would give them some sense of being active agents engaging with processes in relation to their own care generally.

Graham and Bruce model

Children are seen as having:

- Social agency and active participation in social life. This view is central to understanding children's well-being.
- Children from black communities often have few opportunities to narrate their lived experiences in public institutions including child welfare.

- Children are listened to within broader social contexts that include their lived experiences of difference.
- Active participation in decision-making activities can accord both recogniton and protection. This approach can offer a sense of being active agents engaging with the processes in relation to their own care generally.

Source: Graham and Bruce (2006)

Bernard (2002) considers the complex processes by which black children give voice to parental maltreatment and the ways in which societal racism frames their understanding and gives meaning to their experiences. These processes are particularly significant in the light of the Victoria Climbié Inquiry, which identified failures among several professionals to engage with Victoria to uncover her dreadful life circumstances (Laming, 2003). Victoria's aunt, Marie-Thérèse Kouao, brought her to England from the Ivory Coast in the hope of a good education and a better life. Over the course of a year, Victoria suffered appalling injuries that led to her death in 2000. The subsequent public inquiry made known the consistent failure of professionals to undertake home visits to challenge her suspected abusers. The inaction of professionals extended to Victoria's stay in hospital where although her injuries were recognised as non-accidental she was then diagnosed as having scabies and returned to her aunt. The inability of social services to protect children known to them has been a consistent feature of child abuse inquiries for many years. The lack of communication within and between agencies continues to be a critical factor indicating organisational failures as well as practice issues.

Rustin (2005, p 16), in her article about the critical moments in Victoria Climbié's life, looks at the political and social context surrounding the failure of professionals to protect her. She asks "was her black skin a source of fear to some (linked to the theme of contamination) ... and also an excuse for politically correct but mindless thoughts about cultural differences in child care which could set to rest the alarming observations of her terrorized obedience when Kouao was present?". Rustin brings to light the wider and disturbing aspects about the representations of black children as asylum-seekers in desperate need: "in Victoria's mind she may indeed have come to see herself as someone who was a recipient of 'Action Aid', appalling as that had turned out to be" (Rustin, 2005, p 16). Victoria Climbié, a black African child, although not hidden from the view of welfare professionals, can be perceived as the 'other', an outsider and asylum-seeker. These images are often presented in the context of media campaigns against asylum-seekers and 'immigrants' and discussions about their entitlement to social welfare services. These representations of a black child as the 'other' were further compounded by the disputed diagnosis of scabies leading to the refusal of the police and social workers to visit her.

The Laming Report (2003) also considered instances where professionals failed to appreciate how language could be manipulated in certain situations (Chand, 2005). It was recorded that "Marie-Thérèse presented as smart in appearance, proud and a woman who articulated very well". However, her grasp of the English language would fail her whenever she was asked specific child protection questions: "Then she appeared not to understand, was evasive and would turn to the interpreter for support" (Laming, 2003, p 152).

Engaging and listening to children is regarded as a critical aspect of professional practice, particularly in the area of child abuse. Although it was clear that Victoria Climbié spoke some English, it was not her first language, and therefore the process of 'telling' was particularly difficult. For black children who do not speak English, there are many disadvantages in the process of disclosure, not least because they are unable to disclose abuse or speak about their lives except through interpreters. This can be problematic because interpreters "belong to the same communities and will be affected by the same tensions and dilemmas" (Webb et al, 2002, p 402).

Garrett (2004) considers that Victoria Climbié fulfilled the role of a 'traditional' child in that she was seen, but rarely heard or spoken to in her first language, by those professionals charged with safeguarding her welfare. Here her best interests would have been served by focusing on her experiences rather than the intent of her carers. Bernard (2002, p 249) also looks at the process of 'telling' and the difficulties of voicing experiences for some black children. Bernard emphasises the need "to be able to hear what black children are telling us, and perhaps more importantly, paying attention to the silences surrounding what they are not telling us is a crucial component of risk assessment" (p 249). These insights require efforts for a more informed understanding of the process of silencing and the urgent need to make visible the needs and concerns of children who have remained hidden, to secure their well-being within the context of societal racism.

Every Child Matters: 2004 Children Act

Under the auspices of *Every Child Matters* (DfES, 2004), these new proposals mark a shift in social policy in positioning children in the centre stage of the policy process (Williams, 2004). As well as proposing a more universal approach to children along the lines of multidisciplinary provision, the importance of children having a voice is acknowledged. The aftermath of the Victoria Climbié Inquiry forms the backdrop in these new proposals to make visible children who have remained hidden and most vulnerable to social exclusion by providing a wider and more integrative approach to children's services. These new proposals led to the passage of the 2004 Children Act, providing the legislative framework to reform and develop children's services. The Act outlines five main outcomes for children and young people:

- being healthy
- staying safe
- enjoying and achieving
- making a positive contribution
- economic well-being.

These outcomes for children move away from a focus solely on children in need to a wider vision of assisting all children together with providing more accessible holistic services in local communities. The Act places emphasis on providing universal services for children that integrate both targeted and specialist provision with a focus on early intervention and better prevention. These policy documents link with the government's agenda on social exclusion because they widen provisions for children with more emphasis on successful preventative services:

> Every child having an opportunity to fulfil their potential.
> And no child slipping through the net. (DfES, 2004, p 5)

By expanding children's services to include the development of participative preventative services, the Act shifts policy and practice from 'children in need' to 'children at risk'. This preventative agenda recognises that children are among those adversely affected by the impacts of social exclusion. This framework gives attention to multiagency working and local collaborative arrangements to bring together services for children. However, although these developments are welcomed, preventing social exclusion needs to be understood within the context of children's lives and their social positioning in the wider society.

It is now widely recognised that children experience different kinds of childhoods and to understand what it means to be a black child in the context of societal racism requires understanding of the broader social and political backgrounds that influence their opportunities and life chances. For example, black children enter the public care system based on an individualised, liberal, ethnocentric notion of children's welfare and well-being. In these institutions the focus is directed towards the needs of individual children largely divorced from their social contexts that not only disallows their collective identities, but also promotes their shared processes of marginalisation, historical neglect and differential treatment as irrelevant (Krieken, 1999). So, in relation to the complex relations between children and institutions, black children are subject to formal and informal hierarchies in society that shape and influence children's lives (Graham and Bruce, 2006).

Williams (2004) welcomes many aspects of this long-term programme, not least because these proposals show a commitment towards developing earlier identification of children in need and represent a new seriousness towards children's agency and participation. In their analysis of *Every Child Matters*, Daniel et al (2005) make the case for approaches that recognise that policies may impact differently on children according to their gender and to promote gender equity. Equally important, *Every Child Matters* must develop policies and encourage research agendas that bring black and minority ethnic children into view to ensure their voices are heard.

Conclusion

This chapter has set out a range of complex issues in working with black families and children. Models of race relations including assimilation and 'colour-blind' approaches framed early perspectives and social work practice. It was the high presence of black children in care that brought issues of race and social work to public attention. Issues of power and institutional racism and neglect underpinned many of the issues that came into view.

Although there were some bitter confrontations between black communities and social services, it was black-led efforts that played an important role in changing social work policy and practice. As social work evolved with an emphasis on working in partnership with clients, empowerment and strengths models of practice seemed more appropriate and useful for black families and children. By incorporating resilience factors, the voices of marginalised groups could be integrated into social work practice. The 1989 Children Act introduced a duty on child welfare agencies to consider issues of culture, language and religion that has placed these issues firmly within a legal framework. However, some 16 years after the implementation of the Act, these issues tend to be neglected in social work research (Graham, 2006a).

Issues of identity and the quality of care of black children brought into view the identity needs of all children and the importance of retaining contact with communities, family and friends. This chapter has provided an overview of the legislation governing leaving care and highlighted the needs of young black people that are often not addressed adequately. Listening to young black people to understand and take into account their wider experiences of discrimination is an important aspect of practice. By building on recognition of their social achievements, these protective factors can assist young people who often struggle to find opportunities to talk about their lived experiences and positive ways to manage life experiences.

In the last section of this chapter I presented an overview of issues concerning child abuse and black families. The tragic case of Victoria Climbié has again brought attention to flawed professional practices and the lack of interagency working. Another related issue considered in this chapter is the social position of black children in the wider society and its impact on their lives. Young black people leaving care continue to experience underachievement in education and high levels of unemployment and these multiple disadvantages are inadequately addressed in service provision and practice generally. There is no disagreement that every child in difficult circumstances is entitled to support; however, a greater appreciation of the wider social contexts that hinder the opportunities and well-being of black children is needed to ensure positive and beneficial outcomes.

FIVE

Mental health

Introduction

Mental health is an integral part of overall health and well-being. It has many definitions but is generally described as a "positive sense of well-being and a belief in our own worth and the worth of others" (HEA, 1997, p 2). Having positive mental health means being able to live life to its full potential, to be able to cope with change, the ability to understand and make sense of surroundings. This important aspect of overall health shapes life experiences and is something that individuals, groups and communities aspire to achieve. It is widely accepted that many people experience mental health problems at some point during their lives. Sometimes these problems are sufficiently serious that they require professional intervention and support. People usually seek the help and advice of their local GP as the first point of contact with mental health services leading to a range of professionals, including social workers that may become involved.

Over the years social work has struggled to create mental health as a specialist area of practice with a clear professional identity. With the introduction of community care and the modernising agenda for social services, social workers now have an important role in caring for people with mental health problems as part of community mental health teams. One of the most controversial areas in mental health has been the high presence of black and minority ethnic people who are compulsorily detained in mental health facilities and their experiences of mental health services generally. In this regard, research evidence concludes that black people experience discrimination in mental health services and often receive a service that fails to address their mental health needs (Raleigh, 2000).

It is generally accepted that black people experience racism on an individual, institutional and cultural level in their everyday lives. These are potential sources of stress (stress is defined here as psychological discomfort in living) that can adversely affect their mental health in various ways. For example, differential access to resources, poor housing conditions, discrimination, exclusion and cultural stereotypes can compromise the well-being of black people generally (Williams and

Williams-Morris, 2000).These forms of discrimination can contribute to stress on an individual basis and often have a negative impact on the quality of life.Apart from experiences of hostility, there are routine and subtle forms of differential treatment in everyday life in which black people often experience less respect or receive poorer services.These negative experiences can contribute to repressed anger and one of the key factors here is how individuals manage these unpleasant experiences and what personal resources and support systems are available to them. Many black people have developed protective mechanisms and forms of resistance that they draw on to mitigate these stressors and mostly perceive these experiences as daily annoyances.

Another related but different point is that both psychiatry and psychology are embedded in social ideals and values that determine and limit the distribution of psychiatric care.This means that the perceptions concerning mental health problems and boundaries about what is normal and abnormal behaviour are largely culturally bound. There are long-standing critiques of psychiatry and in particular the use of treatments such as electroconvulsive shock therapy and medications that it is claimed are a sophisticated means of limiting a person's freedom and 'normalising' their behaviour.

Against this background, both psychiatry and psychology have a historical legacy of racism built on white dominance and imperialism (Howitt and Owusu-Bempah, 1990).Widely accepted racist beliefs were transferred into the early development of psychiatry and psychology. These biological-based theories known as 'scientific racism' dominated and directed the development of these disciplines.White norms were set as the standard by which others were judged and researched.These points are important in understanding the context in which there is evidence of misdiagnosis and differential treatment in relation to black people in the mental health system.

With respect to issues of mental health, it is important to look at the terminology used and terms in current usage in the social work literature. People who are experiencing mental health problems are most commonly referred to as the 'patient', 'client', 'service user', 'consumer' and 'survivor'. All these terms are allied to a particular role of people with mental health problems and their relationships with professionals. In this chapter 'mental health problems' are referred to and the term 'service user' or 'client' is used.

This chapter opens with the background and context of mental health policy. It then looks at issues and concerns surrounding black people and discrimination in mainstream mental health services. As major initiatives in the mental health system have taken place, service user groups and their views and concerns have started to become known. Following these discussions, racism in psychology is looked at and the development of black psychology. The next section looks at alternative healing practices and ways of offering support within a cultural and spiritual context. Many societies look to the spiritual dimensions of human experiences to help people cope with mental distress and offer faith and hope as an important factor in their recovery.

Background and context – mental health and key policy responses

The historical background of mental health policy has seen major shifts from asylum care to community care, resulting in different approaches to understanding and dealing with mental health problems that have implications for social work. There are two key approaches that frame thinking about mental health policy and practice that have shaped the development of services and care of people with mental health problems.

First, the biomedical approach has historically dominated mental health interventions with an emphasis on controlling symptoms with medication. This model identifies mental illness as a separate entity to be treated and this approach is implemented by psychiatric and medical services. It is the only branch of medicine that can restrict an individual's freedom largely based on ideas of 'in the best interests of' individuals and society. Before community care, psychiatric services were carried out in institutional settings where reports of abuse and dehumanising practices revealed the negative effects of institutionalisation and the loss of personal autonomy. The work of Goffman (1961) revealed the social organisation of mental asylums that appeared to be oriented towards the needs of the staff rather than the people in these institutions. Even though there has been a shift from institutional care to community care it does not mean that mental health problems have been redefined in a social context because behavioural control continues to be the dominant mode of treatment. Clearly, there are limitations in adopting a purely medical approach in the field of mental health since it does not deal with feelings, emotions, anxieties and fears. Moreover, this model tends to isolate individuals from their family and social environment and ignores the impact of social contexts in mental breakdown. Social workers in community health teams bring a unique understanding about mental health processes at a macro-societal level that helps to counterbalance the weight placed on biomedical approaches.

Second, the social model approach favours the psychosocial contexts of mental health problems with an emphasis on collaboration with service users, participation and empowerment. This model has attracted attention in recent years as social factors and the impact of environment are recognised as highly influential in people developing mental health problems. Social workers operating from this approach seek to support as well as care for people with mental health problems on the road to recovery.

After the introduction of community care in the early 1990s, people with mental health problems in long-term facilities were discharged into the community where they could be offered services to support their care. Within the NHS mental health services are often described as the 'Cinderella service'. This description points to the long-term neglect and lack of investment in the development of mental health services fit for the 21st century. Mental health services have lagged behind other areas of the NHS, and in 2001 the Department of Health described mental health services as having "shabby and depressing wards that would never have been tolerated in medicine or surgery" (DH, 2001a, p 4).

There have been ongoing difficulties in providing a comprehensive and integrated mental health service based in the community that have led to complaints of inadequate care and support. Alongside these problems, there has been mounting criticism in the media due to high profile cases of violent attacks by individuals suffering from acute mental problems and the lack of supervision of people with mental health problems. Consequently, people with mental health problems have been linked to violent behaviour and possible risks involved to the general public. Despite research evidence to the contrary, images of people with mental health problems as potential 'maniacs' waiting to attack unsuspecting passers-by have been fuelled by the media, entering public debate and concern. However, people with mental health problems are more likely to be victims than perpetrators of violent behaviour (Lester and Glasby, 2006).

The 1983 Mental Health Act introduced an approved social worker status with specialist training to undertake the assessment, support and monitoring functions in communities and residential settings. During the assessment process, practitioners work with clients to prepare a social history of the client that includes personal, family and social factors. Here, issues of racism and appropriate needs can be identified together with developing partnerships with family and friends in the interests of people with mental health problems. Having a relative with mental health problems often affects family relationships and close friends in many different ways. Practitioners can assist families in understanding and supporting their loved ones and act as a link or bridge between specialist services and an individual's social context and environment.

Social workers are empowered to protect civil rights and to ensure that legislation is applied properly. Social workers often practise in crisis situations and play an important role in deciding the best course of action to take for people with mental health problems. Practitioners can consider various options for intervention including counselling, group work and family work and are responsible for coordinating assessments for compulsory admission. Social workers are the only professionals that have a statutory requirement to show understanding of practice in a multicultural society. Although there have been some initiatives in the training of doctors, nurses and police, there is no statutory requirement in these professions to demonstrate anti-discriminatory practice, awareness of cultural issues or cultural sensitivity. Reid-Galloway (2002, p 4) maintains that "it is this failure to incorporate an understanding of the significance of race and culture into a systematic professional response which makes the diagnosis or assessment procedure unreliable and highly stressful".

Since the 1983 Act, social workers have faced further changes in legislation, organisational policy and practice. Gaps in existing patterns of services and failure to meet the needs of service users contributed to policy changes and initiatives to modernise mental health services. In responding to these concerns, the *National Service Framework for mental health* (DH, 1999) set out a vision of a more holistic approach to mental health practice that would directly address issues of discrimination, social exclusion and partnership with service users. In this document the Labour government recognised the need to give more attention to mental health services overall and in particular raise standards in the care and treatment of people with mental health problems.

The *National Service Framework for mental health* also calls for professionals to develop knowledge and skills to demonstrate cultural competence in working with diverse communities. These improvements in services would place emphasis on social perspectives and integrate social work with other professions to provide a seamless service. This framework for mental health includes provision for preventative services to reduce the incidence of mental health problems in the first place. One of the priorities recognised in these new initiatives is to reduce the stigma and discrimination that surrounds mental health problems. This requires professionals to provide ongoing support and assistance to break down the barriers that lead to social exclusion.

National Service Framework for mental health: modernising mental health services

The National Service Framework recommends that people with mental health problems should be able to expect that services will:

Involve service users and their carers in planning and delivery of care

Deliver high quality treatment and care that is known to be effective and appropriate

Be well suited to those who use them and non-discriminatory

Be accessible so that help can be obtained when and where it is needed

Promote their safety and that of their carers, staff and the wider public

Offer choices that promote independence

Be well coordinated between all staff and agencies

Deliver continuity of care for as long as this is needed

Empower and support their staff

Be properly accountable to the public, service users and carers.

Source: DH (1999)

Currently, mental health policy tends to be dominated by risk assessment and public safety issues that emphasise the need for careful monitoring of risky individuals with mental health problems and the risk they may pose to communities. Many authors, however, argue that issues concerning users' rights, needs and experiences of services are downplayed or receive much less attention (Beresford and Croft, 2002).

Since the late 1970s the disparities between black communities and the majority population in the rates of mental health problems and mental healthcare services have been the subject of many research studies and reports, yet little has changed. Why are black men of African Caribbean background six times more likely to be compulsorily detained than the majority population? Why are Asian women more vulnerable to depression and why are both groups less likely to seek early help from primary care (Golightley, 2004)? Since the 1970s, these questions continue to be the subject of many articles and discussions in mental health.

There are several explanations given for these disparities and routes into the mental health system. One of the most compelling explanations is the impact of adverse environmental circumstances on both material and social interactions and their links to mental health problems. It is suggested that some groups in society are more vulnerable to mental health problems because there are both material and psychological consequences of social injustice and oppression. Black people have long narrated the impact of environmental pressures on mental health and well-being. Sheppard (2002) solicits the views of African Caribbean mental health users on the causes of mental health problems. They referred to experiences of growing up in a hostile environment, with few positive, and many negative, images of black people, the alienating nature of the education system, and problems of adolescence and stress. It is in this context that black people tend to be over-represented across mental health institutions (US DHHS, 2001; Bhuik, 2002; DH, 2003).

Racism as a spiral of oppression

Black people in society may respond to racism in different ways, for example, by countering it, accepting it, adapting to it or internalising it. All of these may to a greater or lesser extent cause emotional distress, because of constantly having to challenge racism, often with seemingly little effect.

The experience of being excluded from the benefits of mainstream society and made to feel inferior; constantly having to juggle identity in order to be accepted; and having to deny cultural identity with a consequent fragmenting of the sense of self contributes to a spiral of oppression.

Source: Adapted from Bhuik (2002, p 212)

Bhuik (2002) maintains that experiences of everyday racism, both subtle and overt, more often than not cause emotional distress and play a key role in compromising the well-being of black people generally. This means individuals have to draw on internal and personal resources to deal with these experiences within the context of life's ups and downs. Some individuals may not have the resources or support systems in place to mitigate these painful experiences and may go on to develop mental health problems. This situation takes individuals into the mental health system that is a product of society by virtue of its ideals and Eurocentric norms and values. Bhuik (2002) claims that moving into the mental health system as it currently stands can compound mental distress because it tends to reproduce racism on an institutional and individual level. Following this assertion, the mental health system often ignores racism as a factor in the development of mental health problems in the first place.

Another explanation often suggested for the high presence of black people in psychiatric facilities is the possible misdiagnosis of mental health conditions by psychiatrists. Fernando (2001) asks the question "Do psychiatric diagnoses and treatments carry the racial bias against black people prevalent in western culture?". Does black anger or protest against white domination get presented as high rates of diagnosed 'illnesses', such as schizophrenia, that carry anger within them? The lack of awareness of the impact of racism and cultural differences among many psychiatrists together with few black psychiatrists can lead to misdiagnosis. The issues of anti-discriminatory practice and cultural competence need to be addressed in the training of psychiatrists and other professionals involved in mental health practice. Fernando (2001, p 109) considers that "although there is some concern in Britain about racism in psychiatry, this has not led to the adoption of any particular strategies to counteract it.... However, the challenges to both psychiatry and psychology are increasing, particularly from users of psychiatric services and from ... organisations run by black and Asian people". Fernando considers that in this context mainstream psychiatry and psychology cannot carry on with a 'business as usual' attitude and that radical change is required to address these issues.

Black people and mental health services

One of the overriding issues in mental health services has been the failure to recognise the needs of different individuals and communities. This 'colour-blind' approach has been a constant feature of the welfare state because of its commitment to provide a universal service where everyone has equal access to the same service. This overarching principle in effect means that "the services which the welfare state provides have often been designed from the point of view of dominant groups of people within society" (Lester and Glasby, 2006, p 178). Consequently, the needs of black people with mental health problems have been neglected or marginalised even though there is a high presence of black people in mental health services. It is currently acknowledged by the Department of Health that the experiences of black people with mental health problems and the poor levels of support and inadequate care they receive may even be getting worse (DH, 2003).

As the high presence of black people and in particular young black men (of African Caribbean background) detained in psychiatric institutions became widely known, issues of discrimination, inappropriate care and gaps in services began to surface. In 1997, the Mental Health Act Commission reported that:

> ... provision for patients from ethnic minority communities often remains basic, insensitive, and piecemeal, leading to patients feeling alienated and isolated. It is dispiriting that the serious issue of inappropriate care and treatment of patients from Black and ethnic minority communities which were raised in previous biennial reports continue to cause concern and to be noted in reports of commission visits.

Wilson (2001, p 35) sets out the disparities and major concerns about black people and the mental health system in the following way. Black people are more likely to be:

- referred to psychiatric services via the police or judicial system;
- removed by the police to a place of safety under section 136 of the 1983 Mental Health Act; this section of the Act gives police powers to detain an individual for up to 72 hours;
- detained in hospital under sections 2, 3 and 4 of the Act;
- diagnosed as suffering from schizophrenia or other forms of psychotic illness;
- detained in a locked ward of psychiatric hospitals;
- given higher doses of medication and to be medicated intramuscularly (Reid–Galloway, 2002).

Black people are also less likely to receive treatment at an early stage or receive treatments such as psychotherapy or counselling. Although most of these issues were identified largely in relation to the African Caribbean community, mental health has been the subject of growing concern within Asian communities with similar experiences in mental healthcare. Wilson (2001) considers the impact of racism across these communities and the tensions associated with living in a racist society that can be a draining and wearing influence in black people's lives.

Racial harassment within mental health settings was also identified as a problem that black people often faced during their detention in mental health institutions. This form of discrimination prompted the NHS to mount a campaign to end racial harassment. Racial harassment was also implicated in the recent death of David Bennett in psychiatric care after he was forcibly restrained by staff face down on the floor for about 25 minutes. This tragic death raised questions about dehumanising practices and racial abuse in mainstream mental health settings. Lester and Glasby (2006, p 190) suggest that "Bennett may have been one of at least twenty seven 'black' people since 1980 to die while in psychiatric services".

Keating and Robertson (2004) maintain there are 'circles of fear' surrounding interactions between black people and professionals in mental health services. In the context of societal racism, in relationships between service users and professionals black people more often than not are perceived as a threat or dangerous. Keating and Robertson believe that some professionals are fearful of black people and that in turn affects many professionals' ability to engage effectively with service users. These fears emerge from racist stereotypes prevalent in the wider society about black people generally. Barnes and Bowl (2001) argue that popular media images of young black men as 'big, black and dangerous' have entered the imagination of the public, including practitioners. These images are not new, but have recently become part of a strong racist undercurrent in public debate about mental health. As a result of these poor interactions and mistrust, it is not surprising that black people often regard mental health services with suspicion and trepidation (Sayce, 1995).

Keating and Robertson (2004) describe the care pathways and experiences of black service users as problematic. They point out that "black communities associate mental illness with being detained in hospital and involuntary treatment in a confined and restrictive environment ... such is the level of disenchantment with services amongst service users and families and carers that there is a feeling that services no longer have the best interests of clients at heart" (p 440).

Many black mental health service users do not believe mainstream mental health services can offer positive help and say they receive services they do not want and not the ones they do or might want. For Keating and Robertson (2004), breaking down the circles of fear is the first step in making improvements in mental health service delivery. This can be achieved by systematic change in the experiences of service users at each point in the care pathway. Taking these issues further, some commentators have suggested a dual approach both inside and outside the mental health system. This requires making mental health services more appropriate through working for change inside the mental health system itself, while at the same time building capacity within black communities and the voluntary sector. These strategies are outlined in the National Institute for Mental Health in England report entitled *Inside outside: Improving mental health services for black and minority ethnic communities* (DH, 2003). However, Lester and Glasby (2006) are cautious in following this line of strategies because of the danger of marginalising black people through specialist services while leaving mainstream services untouched. Above all, services must be of good quality and responsive to the needs of all service users irrespective of their backgrounds.

Black mental health service users

As mental health policy has moved up the political agenda, new approaches and improvements to services have increased awareness among professionals of a more holistic approach to mental health. These new approaches include the participation of service users in the delivery of mental health services. In recent years, the perspectives and concerns of service users have emerged as an important aspect of social work and social care. The new arrangements under the 1990 Community Care Act reshaped social work tasks into care management that involved other professionals including occupational therapists and nurses. As organisational changes took hold, recipients of social services were redefined as consumers. Participation of service users was introduced based on a consumerist agenda with importance placed on gathering feedback about available services from users.

Beresford and Croft (2002) maintain that these initial exercises in canvassing feedback from service users have had very limited effects on improving their lives or services. In fact, many service user groups reported that there was too much consultation and effort on the part of the groups to provide information that has resulted in largely stressful and unproductive experiences. Beresford and Croft (2002, p 388) recount that "there is now a strong and growing sense of 'consultation fatigue' and distrust of agency initiatives for involvement among service users and their organisations. They do not see themselves in narrow terms as 'consumers' of social work or 'users' of social services".

Since the 1980s the drive for a stronger role for service users in policy and practice emerged and the mental health users' movements began to make their voices heard. These user-based organisations came about largely through the traditional voluntary sector. For example,

Mind (the National Association for Mental Health) mounted several campaigns to support the end of discrimination towards people with mental health problems in the wider society. They also engaged service users and encouraged their participation in the work of Mind.

Another organisation that exists at a local and national level is Survivors Speak Out, and here people with mental health problems began to identify themselves as survivors. This development has particular importance because of the negative images and language associated with mental illness. Historically, people with mental health problems have been described as 'mad', 'lunatics' and other disparaging terms and their voices rarely heard about the treatment meted out to them. As concerns about individual freedom and challenges to psychiatry and related professions developed, service user groups sought to redefine mental health problems away from illness to adopt a recovery and wellness model with a primary focus on the goals of service users such as employment, independence and a better quality of life.

As these mental health user groups and organisations gained some attention, it became known that black service users were not well represented, and, as Barnes and Bowl (2001, p 90) point out, "given [these] arguments about the particular experiences of black service users, it is perhaps striking on contact with service user movement organisations that there are so few black faces". One of the reasons why black people seem to be under-represented among the service user movement is that the movement itself reflects racist attitudes found in the wider society. A member of a black mental health group in Leicester reported that "I found the patients even more racist than the staff. One of them had the habit of calling me Sambo. I couldn't believe it; even mad people hate us" (Westwood, 1989, p 10).

There is also evidence that for many service users their patient status is their main area of concern and frame of reference. On the other hand, for most black service users their identity as black people is equally important and cannot be ignored because it is through these experiences that most problems need to be understood. Barnes and Bowl (2001, p 91) make the point that "ignoring such differences and placing too much stress on the shared experiences of services, may, therefore, simply serve to alienate black service users".

Although this chapter has painted a rather bleak picture of mental health services so far, black mental health users have outlined six main areas that could be improved:

- information disadvantage – examples reported by people included not knowing their diagnosis or treatment;

- not having access to an interpreter and rights of appeal;
- lack of choice about treatment;
- people wanted more information, and more discussion about treatment, change of medication and access to alternatives;
- not being listened to;
- stopping or reducing medication (Reid-Galloway, 2002).

Empowering black mental health service users

There is growing interest in the recovery model that moves away from traditional outcomes such as compliance and treatment to encompass a way of living that is satisfying and contributing to life even with the limitations caused by mental health problems. The recovery-oriented approach builds on individual strengths and responsibility and views life with purpose and meaning. This means helping individuals who are recovering to develop capacity for self-determination with themes of hope, healing and an emphasis on human rights. There are no fixed definitions of a recovery model that can include a range of approaches. Anthony (1993, p 11) defines recovery in the following way:

> ... a person with mental illness can recover even though the illness is not cured.... Recovery is a way of living and having a satisfying, hopeful and contributing life even with the limitations caused by illness. Recovery involves the development of new meaning and purpose in one's life as one goes beyond the catastrophic effects of mental illness. (quoted in Lester and Glasby, 2006, p 22)

The recovery model encourages self-expression and a sense of pride in achievements and holding onto a life that has a meaning for individuals to enable them to integrate more easily into society. This means listening and engaging with the lived experiences of people with mental health problems so that recovery is about "helping people live the lives they want to lead. And in the service of this, hope and opportunity are central. The professionals' care role must be to help people to hold on to hope" (Perkins, 2003, p 6). Recovery from mental health problems also includes recovery from stigma and discrimination that many people with mental health problems experience in their daily lives.

This model has been taken up by many black voluntary organisations providing services to black communities. These services tend to be user-friendly environments where the service users direct and shape the kinds of services offered. The opinions and views of service users are valued within a culturally holding environment. This framework has much strength not least because there is an understanding of the histories of black people as well as the effects of individual and institutional racism. Social gatherings sometimes referred to as 'reasonings/dialogue', counselling and social activities are central features of this model that includes relatives and friends who seek to assist individuals to achieve a better quality of life in their communities. According to Frederick (1995, p 42):

> ... the issues involved in provision of mental health services are complex ... it will not be as simple as providing the occasional meal of rice, peas and chicken, and adding a few cultural pictures on the walls. Increasing the number of Black faces in face-to-face services will bring improvement but only if there is a proper race perspective in all training courses for staff in mental health and related fields.... Many Black-led organisations are striving to provide alternative models of service ... much of our attention is taken up with looking at coping mechanisms for dealing with an individual's problem and providing support while enhancing self-esteem and nurturing independence.

Views of black service users

How mental health service workers can empower black people in mental health settings:

- acknowledge and value cultural differences;
- accept expressions of culture and spirituality;
- recognise and acknowledge personal and institutional racism as a real feature of black people's lives;
- mental health workers taking responsibility for challenging racist behaviour and comments, whether from staff or other mental health service users;
- recognise institutional and personal racism in psychiatry and how it affects black people;
- recognise that some anger at the oppression experienced within the mental health system is justified and a healthy response to injustice.
- plan and arrange appropriate culturally based services in the community and voluntary sector;

> • recognise the importance and interdependence of family and social networks in the community to overall health and well-being.
>
> *Source:* Adapted from Bhuik (2002, p 81)

Black psychology

The history of racism in psychology has been well documented by several researchers and psychologists (Howitt and Owusu-Bempah, 1990). As mentioned earlier in this chapter, the new science of psychology emerged within the context of European expansion and imperialism during a historical period when differences between human beings were categorised and became a valid area of scientific enquiry. Early developments in psychology and anthropology advanced racist theories that filtered into academic and research literature.

In this context, black scholars have been propelled into considering and advocating a black psychology because of the need to "build a conceptual model to organise, explain and understand the psycho/social behaviour of black people" (White, 1984, p 3). Black psychology emerged in the US during the civil rights movement in the 1960s as a form of resistance to mainstream and traditional psychology. Black psychology examined the psychological consequences of being black in western societies. The early perspectives in black psychology were necessarily reactive and based on critiques of traditional psychology and its involvement in constructing black families as dysfunctional and pathological. Black psychologists, however, have since defined black psychology as a model of liberation and empowerment. The application of this model is more valuable to black people as a way of meaningfully reflecting on social life. Black psychologists seek to have a positive impact on mental health and to address the neglected psychological and spiritual needs of black people.

Nobles (2004) considers a rationale for black psychology as:

- engaging in a critique and rejection of white psychology's methodology and conclusions;
- providing Afrocentric models for study, theory and therapy;
- self-consciously intervening in the struggle for a more humane and just society and environment.

Black psychologists have been frustrated by the lack of commitment and change in mainstream psychology and have decided that the only way to serve their communities is to develop their own theoretical frameworks. This perspective is important because black psychology can explore black subjectivities through appropriate and relevant frameworks. This direction has embraced cultural and liberating dimensions to address the experiences of black people rooted in their histories and philosophies.

Frantz Fanon (1967), one of the first black psychiatrists, produced an in-depth understanding of colonialism and its effects on black people's psychological health and well-being. Fanon claimed that mental distress is not caused by individual pathology but is a response by the individual to the cultural context in which she or he lives. He explored the ways in which European culture undermines a black person's mental health through disrespect for difference. Since humans are vulnerable to psychological injury through insult and disrespect, the experience of disrespect can become a source of motivation for acts of resistance articulated through social movements. Black people in Britain also experience racism as part of a postcolonial experience where they are positioned within defined stereotypes and fantasies in the wider society. These stereotypes and fantasies perceive colonial people as objects of fear, hate and derision.

During the 1970s the field of black psychology moved away from criticising traditional psychology to establishing its own theoretical and therapeutic practice centred on the experience and integrity of black people. Following these developments, black psychologists began to recognise the importance of understanding African philosophy as a framework to inform human functioning and development leading to a growing body of literature (Myers, 1988; Parham, 2002; Nobles, 2004). Using African philosophical principles and lived experiences of black people, black psychologists such as Nobles, Akbar and Myers apply this knowledge to understand the psychology of black people. However, in discussing Afrocentric worldviews Belgrave and Allison (2005, p 28) maintain that:

> Although it is important to note there are variations in the Afrocentric and other worldviews, and individuals may function along a continuum, with some people of African descent having some Eurocentric worldview beliefs and some people of European descent having some Africentric worldview beliefs. However, in general it is expected that [African-centred or] Africentric worldview dimensions will be found in some degree amongst most people of African descent.

Robinson (1995) explores a range of issues in black psychology including families, identities and mental health. Each section of the text applies these issues to social work practice. According to Robinson (1995), an understanding of black perspectives in psychology can assist social workers in assessing black people with mental health difficulties with more accuracy. In this way, social workers can study what is effective for black people on their own terms building on their strengths and coping skills. This set of strategies avoids making comparisons with the majority population and instead places emphasis on lived experiences and cultural themes and products as routes to healing and recovery (Graham, 2005).

The development of black psychology has not been without its critics. Some black psychologists have pointed to the shortcomings of black psychology because it can perpetuate the idea that there is a homogeneous black experience. This leads to a tendency to assume that there is one reality of racism and experience of being black in British society. Black psychology also tends to generate similar criticisms that are apparent in feminist psychology in that race issues become the overriding frame of reference that may exclude other differences such as gender and social background.

In the meantime, black psychology has taken a cultural turn in recent years and become part of a larger movement in psychology that is known as cross-cultural psychology (Belgrave and Allison, 2005). These developments have been useful for social workers and other care professionals in advancing culturally competent theory and practice. With an emphasis on culturally diverse practice, social workers seek to engage with the role of culture as well as issues of oppression in the helping relationship.

Alternative and holistic approaches to mental health and well-being

In recent years there has been a trend towards an understanding of a holistic approach to mental health and well-being. This trend appears to be in response to some of the many limitations of conventional medicine and healthcare. Moodley and West (2005, p xx) note the "paradox of contemporary western healing practices that appear to be so sophisticated and underpinned by postmodern technology, yet patients are turning to traditional healing methods". Moreover, the medical model is not sufficient in promoting optimal health and well-being. In contemporary society many people are actively seeking alternative treatments for physical ailments that draw on traditional healing practices, for example, acupuncture, herbalism, yoga, massage and meditation.

These traditional healing methods take a holistic approach to well-being that provides alternative ways of dealing with ill health. Conventional psychology is based on the assumption that the mind and body are separate entities that tends to form a disembodied understanding of mental processes. This means that the mind is perceived as superior to the body and this exclusive focus on the mind as a separate entity underplays the importance of the physical and spiritual dimensions of being. Many cultures throughout the world hold different approaches to human behaviour and well-being and have developed explanations for human behaviour as well as culturally specific ways of dealing with human problems and distress (Sue, 2006).

Most societies have people who are designated as healers to give comfort to people who are experiencing problems of living. For example, in some cultures the shaman is a healer who is perceived to have powers beyond the senses. Some of these healing practices have been reformulated and reconstituted in various ways by black communities. Black people sometimes consult healers within their own communities and these healers are perceived as qualified practitioners providing a valuable service. However, there are some 'healers' who are dubious and likely to practise 'quackery' so there are risks involved in approaching a healer who is unknown within a community.

Approaches to healing and counselling include spiritual dimensions that drive healing practices towards well-being. This is because it is believed that there are spiritual dimensions to social problems and living. The task of all living things is to maintain balance in the face of adverse external social forces. King (1994, p 20) explains that "being in harmony with life means that one is living with life – co-operating with natural forces that influence events and experiences while simultaneously taking responsibility for one's life by consciously choosing and negotiating the direction and paths one will follow".

Accordingly, when inner peace is compromised, the psychological, social and physical well-being of a person is threatened. Illness and mental health problems are seen as an imbalance or a separation between elements and the healer seeks to restore balance and harmony. As Sue (2006, p 215) explains, "both the ancient Chinese practice of acupuncture and chakras in Indian yoga philosophy involve the use of subtle matter to rebalance and heal the body and mind". Spirituality has played a central role in traditional healing practices in many black communities and it is believed that the spiritual dimensions of human experiences can assist people to cope with mental distress and offer faith as an important factor in their recovery. There is a belief in the unity of spirit, mind and body and the spiritual plane has significance across all areas of life and is pivotal to human development and communication with others. Spirituality is closely associated with emotional well-being. Through our understanding of the spiritual self we come to recognise and appreciate human emotions as an energy force. Spirituality is a key element in the well-being of individuals and reflects the human need to connect to the life force which can "give power and strength in physical communication as a means of connecting the inner strengths and character to the outer existence and collective identity" (Dei, 1999, p 6).

These ways of healing and offering support are sometimes ridiculed as primitive superstition or 'magic' (Fernando, 2001). It is largely the case that traditional healing practices do not command respect and are perceived as unscientific – a kind of 'mumbo-jumbo' in comparison to western 'scientific' psychiatry. This rigid stance is short-sighted because there are many lessons to learn from older forms of healing and western forms of counselling have been slow to acknowledge the existence of these practices. Integral to these issues are relations of power that work to sideline or negate the worldviews of black communities in understanding human behaviour. However, culturally specific and traditional healing therapies continue to be an important medium for healing and well-being in many communities (Graham, 2005).

In a study of indigenous healing in 16 countries, Lee et al (1992) report that three approaches to healing were used. First, communal groups and family networks were used to shelter the disturbed individual and engage in group problem solving; second, spirituality, religious beliefs and community traditions framed the healing process; and, third, the use of shamans who were perceived to be the keepers of traditional wisdom, healing and understanding (Sue, 2006).

Spirituality and social work

Spirituality and social work continue to have an uneasy relationship. This is because spirituality is often closely tied to religious beliefs. Although the history of social work has been strongly influenced by Judaeo-Christian religious traditions that have shaped its development, the process of secularisation and the possibility of religious bias have dampened professional interest generally in reviving the links between religion and social work. However, despite the absence of spirituality in many social work texts, the spiritual dimension of life experience continues to be an important element of helping processes.

In recent years the profession has been reviewing its use of spirituality in practice. In the wake of this renewed interest, it is argued that spirituality is not necessarily based on religious affiliations. Therefore, people may choose to express their spirituality in various ways that are devoid of religious considerations. Bullis (1996) argues that there is a need to consider spirituality in social work and offers the following rationale. First, social work and spirituality are closely linked in promoting common interests and self-respect. Spirituality embraces personal and social healing that is in line with the helping processes in social work. Moreover, spirituality is dedicated to process and can assist social work models of intervention to function more effectively in modern society. In this way, spirituality and social work can learn from each other in promoting personal and social transformation (Graham, 2002).

Second, spiritual knowledge can assist social workers to know and understand the spiritual dimensions of a person's worldview in devising helping strategies within assessment processes. The spiritual dimensions of life often become accentuated when human beings are confronted with life difficulties. Human beings are social beings and for many people purpose gives meaning in their lives. For many people purpose and meaning are located in their communities as this is where meaning and purpose evolve with reference to and in encounters with others (Wells Irme, 1984). In this way, spiritual values can give meaning to life experiences and insights into the possibilities inherent within the helping process. Third, as social workers are likely to come into contact with culturally diverse clients, it is important to have an appreciation of older healing systems as well as potential conflicts in belief systems.

Conclusion

Over time the experience of black people in mental health services has raised many issues, some of which remain overlooked. Mainstream services operate a colour-blind approach that may appear on the surface to be non-discriminatory but in effect pays little attention to the needs and aspirations of black people. Moreover, evidence suggests that they receive by and large a poorer level of support and often inadequate care. Recent developments in service user participation have brought into sharp relief the experiences of black service users and more attention has been given to the delivery of appropriate services. The new standards for mental health have been welcomed because they acknowledge the need for black individuals and organisations to be involved in the planning and delivery of mental health services and take forward some of the demands for change.

In considering recent plans to amend the 1983 Mental Health Act, many commentators have called for the inclusion of the 2000 Race Relations (Amendment) Act to address issues of direct and indirect racism in mental health institutions. These reforms provide a window of opportunity to tackle head-on long-standing adverse institutional and professional practices to address issues of racism in mental health institutions to ensure better outcomes for black mental health users. People with mental health problems have welcomed a more holistic approach to well-being and many organisations have taken on board the recovery model that appears to provide a more integrated approach to support people in the community. This model builds on strengths within individuals, families and communities.

SIX

Disability

Introduction

Social citizenship rights have never been fully extended to disabled people and, as a result of this, disabled people are over-represented among the unemployed and experience higher rates of poverty and in general do not enjoy a standard of living that is comparable with current social expectations. Over time there has been an uneasy relationship between healthcare professionals and disabled people. Professional social work has operated from a framework that encourages paternalism and dependency as part of an individualised understanding of disability. Social work services concerned with disabled people developed in the health sector of the welfare state as well as some services in the voluntary sector. Prior to the 1970 Chronically Sick and Disabled Persons Act, services were frequently provided in a haphazard way. This legislative framework established responsibility for disability services within local authorities. However, the development of services varied across local authorities and tended to be given lower priority than other services.

Social work continues to be dominated by an individual approach or a medical model of disability that has been heavily criticised by disability organisations. Much of the criticism levelled against social work has been the exercise of professional dominance and control over the lives of disabled people that seemed to serve the interests of welfare professionals rather than meet the needs or aspirations of service users. This way of dealing with disabled people created dependency with little opportunity for service users to have a voice in the planning, design or delivery of services.

However, beginning with legislation such as the 1990 NHS and Community Care Act, there have been moves to reduce professional dominance and dependency through managerialism, the introduction of market principles and social care. This legislation introduced care managers into local authorities to undertake assessment of individual needs and then purchase social care packages. In this way, local authorities became enabling authorities rather than direct care providers.

More recently, there have been policy initiatives to support disabled people in achieving independent living by introducing direct payments that allow service users to purchase their own care services. Although these are welcome changes in the design and delivery of services, the medical model continues to hold sway in the way disabled people are defined and tends to inform some provision and practice. Disability is commonly thought of as a way of describing an individual with a range of impairments or abnormalities in the structure or functioning of the human body.

Following these definitions, practitioners in the helping professions, including social workers, teachers and health providers, have often viewed people with disabilities as tragic individuals or as in some way deficient (Swain et al, 2005). This kind of thinking is reflected in wider society where people with disabilities have historically been subject to negative social attitudes, discriminatory practices and policies.

The social model of disability has been a driving force in changing attitudes and shifting attention to the disabling social structures and practices in society and advocating for social change. Disability movements have pointed to the injustices of treating disabled people as objects of pity and charity and have sought equal citizenship to secure a rights-based approach in social policy that emphasises independent living and self-determination. The disability movement has grown over the years to establish a culture, organisations, knowledge and disability as an academic discipline. There have been demands for social work to adopt a social model based on civil and human rights (Beresford and Croft, 2001). A critical aspect of this campaign is to develop new forms of personal and social support that give control and independence to disabled people.

Black disabled people often experience a marginal status within the disability movement that is reflective of their experiences in the wider society. Double jeopardy or double discrimination has been a popular way of describing the experiences of disabled people from black communities. The notion of double jeopardy stems from being both black and disabled but many black people have recoiled from this interpretation of their experiences because it tends to separate their identity and places them in a framework solely as victims. A different approach advocated by Stuart (1996) is one that describes their experiences as simultaneous oppression that can be experienced in a singular or multiple ways.

Even though the disability movement has been successful in making changes to oppressive models of disability and some inroads in legislative reform, they have been less successful in understanding the specific issues and experiences of black disabled people. In recent years, new research agendas have started looking at disability, social care and ethnicity. This body of literature gives voice to the experiences, needs and aspirations of black disabled people.

Given that disability is socially constructed, this chapter begins by looking at some of the key social policy responses and legislative reforms. The next section looks at the different models of disability that includes issues of culture and implications for social work. There is heavy emphasis on the social model that has been adopted by social work recently and this perspective underpins social policy approaches to support disabled people to live independently. The next section gives an overview of the double jeopardy model that is frequently applied to the experiences of black disabled people and looks at new directions in understanding multiple identities, lived experiences and social work practice. The following section gives an overview of independent living and direct payment schemes.

Background and context: some key policy responses

Definitions of disability play a key role in shaping social attitudes, policies and everyday social interactions towards disabled people. In this context, social policy has defined disability as a problem of dependency that has informed service provision and resulted in the collective avoidance of adaptation to social arrangements in society. Definitions of disability also affect the way disabled people see themselves and the world around them.

In this context, postwar social policy reflected a medical model of disability that concentrated on the individual disabled person rather than on their physical or social environment. The 1944 and 1958 Disabled Persons (Employment) Acts were introduced largely out of sympathy for war veterans disabled while fighting for their country (Oliver, 1990). The Acts were based on the assumption that disabled people cannot be expected to compete for employment with able-bodied people. It was generally agreed that disabled people should be compensated for their misfortune and this led to access to lower status occupations often in segregated or sheltered workshops.

These Acts emphasised assessment, rehabilitation and retraining as it was assumed that most disabilities would be physical as a result of recent war. Employment rehabilitation centres were opened to cater for disabled people and adult training centres for adults with learning difficulties. A register of disabled people was set up together with a three per cent quota system for employers of more than 20 staff. On the face of it, this seemed like a first step towards progressive employment practices. However, the majority of employers never met the three per cent quota and exemption permits were routinely granted. This poor record of implementation of the quota system is compared to higher quotas and greater enforcement in many other European countries.

The 1970 Chronically Sick and Disabled Persons Act was supposed to be the beginning of a new era for disabled people. The Act not only placed a duty on local authorities to promote accessibility in housing and public premises but also established services for disabled people as a local authority responsibility. Oliver and Sapey (2006) suggest that although this Act raised the expectations of disabled people, the new generic departments were unable to provide adequate support services and the Act extended dependency rather than securing rights or opportunities for independent living.

During the 1980s, concerns about the mounting costs of welfare led to major changes in social services and the introduction of a mixed economy of social care. There was particular criticism from disability organisations about the failure of services to meet the needs and aspirations of service users. The 1986 Disabled Persons Act was intended to give a voice to disabled people in the assessment of their needs. In practice, however, important sections of this Act were not implemented and there was little overall improvement in target areas. The 1990 NHS and Community Care Act continued with the theme of reducing professional dominance and dependency creation through a strategy of managerialism. As mentioned in Chapter Two, service providers (social workers) had a duty to act as care managers, purchasing welfare services on behalf of their clients.

Service users were given the right to see and even contribute to their care plans but they had no rights to access particular services. Disabled people were rarely involved in the planning and delivery of services in the way that the legislation requires. Disability organisations have been very critical, arguing that the Act fails to empower service users because they are not direct participants in the market and continue to be subject to the power and control of professionals.

With the growing demands for civil rights from disabled people's organisations, the 1995 Disability Discrimination Act deals with discrimination against disabled people in several areas of life including employment, the provision of goods and services and buying and renting land and property. The Act provides a comprehensive anti-discriminatory approach that has been interpreted as the beginning of a shift away from compensatory measures and towards the right to work, independence and personal responsibility. The Act defines disability in narrow terms as "physical or mental impairment which has substantial and long term adverse effects on people's ability to carry out day-to-day activities" (Bagihole, 1997, p 66).

This definition can be seen as an attempt to promote the medical model of disability because of its emphasis on individual impairment. Although the Act has been welcomed as a first step in promoting the full participation of disabled people, it has also been criticised for its limited protection from direct discrimination with many loopholes and weaknesses. Disabled people have often used the phrase the 'Doesn't Do Anything Act' to describe the Act because it is still legal to discriminate against disabled people as employers can use various justifications in a way that is unlawful in relation to the Sex Discrimination or Race Relations Acts.

A moral model of disability

It is widely accepted that disabled people experience discrimination and fewer opportunities across their lifespan and that this has a deep impact on their quality of life. One way of explaining the causes of discrimination and disadvantage is to provide a framework or model within which disability can be understood. Groce (2005, p 6) maintains "in all societies, individuals with disability are not only recognised as distinct from the general population, but value and meaning also are attached to their condition".

One example of the way society views disability is a moral outlook that stems from ancient and modern religious faiths where disability was often linked to sin and evil or conversely disabled people were pitied and seen in need of care. In the past disability in the family sometimes brought shame on its members because disability was seen as a punishment from a higher being. The moral model portrays disability as a "state of existence in conflict with the very moral and spiritual centre of the universe" (Salsgiver, 2006, p 3).

According to this model, disability can be explained in terms of the loss of the moral essence of the individual. Longmore (1993) explains this idea further: "the cause of disability is then not just wrong doing but wrong living; more deeply still, wrong being. In other words, disability … is explained within a cosmic, moral context". Not all explanations about disability within the moral outlook are entirely negative. Groce (2005) gives an example of Mexican American families who often believe that it is God's will that some children will be born with disabilities. For these 'special' children, God will choose kind parents who will be protective of them. With social changes and the adoption of a secular understanding of charity and social need, moral definitions of disability gave way to a medical model of disability.

Disability and culture

All cultures are complex with many variations existing within groups and caveats attached to meaning and understanding. A note of caution here is that some literature on this subject tends to present general statements about culture leading to simple explanations or information about groups of people. By examining cultures in this way, there is a tendency to look at the group itself rather than the wider conditions within which the group lives. As Andersen and Hill-Collins (2004, p 6) maintain, "a narrow focus on culture tends to ignore social conditions of power, privilege and prestige". A more balanced perspective looks at how racism and sexism, for example, have shaped the experience of groups in society.

Groce (2005) suggests that cultural explanations concerning why a disability has occurred have a bearing on the way disabled people are treated in most societies. Sometimes disability is explained in terms of a moral outlook when it is believed disability is caused through divine displeasure or just bad luck. In some societies the cause of disability can also be attributed to transmission by touch or by sight during pregnancy and there is a fear of giving birth to a disabled child as well as variations in the meanings and value attached to different types of disability. For example, disabled people who are blind may be included and supported whereas disabled people with mental health disabilities may be ignored or shunned. Some beliefs about the causes of disability seem to emerge from the need to determine whether the disabled individual is in some way responsible for their current condition. These ideas may be related to making justifiable demands on families or community resources (Groce, 2005).

A medical model of disability

The medical model or individual approach to understanding disability defines disability in terms of a range of discrete clinical conditions that are the result of a personal tragedy or individual misfortune. Underpinning this approach is the belief that human beings have specific and expected biological structures that operate in definite ways. This view of normality identifies people with physical or mental differences as being disabled because of their abnormal structure or functioning and therefore they are characterised as lacking or deficient.

The medical model emphasises the features of the body as a medical condition that needs to be cured or reduced in some way and this belief has been used to justify the exclusion of disabled people from society.

From a historical perspective, the medical model of disability stems from an era when it was believed that human beings could be perfect through fixed notions of normality. This set of ideas has guided scientific progress in the medical profession. While there have been important breakthroughs in understanding the human body and subsequent treatment of illnesses, disability is largely a long-term social state that is not curable.

As the medical model in practice defined people with disabilities in terms of their biological inadequacies, this approach encouraged paternalism and an outlook that people with disabilities are incompetent to manage their own lives. As this model relies on the intervention of professionals, with an emphasis on the disabled body, it tends to downplay disabled people's views and concerns (Salsgiver, 2006). Oliver (1996) claims that it was the concept of need that opened the way for the professional domination of welfare provision. From this perspective, it can be argued that the welfare state has in effect infringed on the citizenship rights of disabled people and undermined their welfare, for example, through the operation of a segregated education system that socialises disabled children into low expectations and fails to equip them with the skills and qualifications they need to compete for places in higher education and in the labour market.

Welfare professionals took charge of disabled people's lives, making decisions for them about their needs and controlling the resources made available to them. The choices available to individuals were limited to the options provided and approved by 'expert' professionals. As a result of this process, disabled people became coerced into passivity and accepting of services even if they were inappropriate.

According to this frame of reference, problems of living that disabled people experience are a direct consequence of their impairment rather than any other explanation, with an onus placed on disabled people to adapt to the way society is organised and not vice versa. Individuals are encouraged to make the best of their situation and to accept limitations. This model of disability has been particularly influential in shaping models of social work practice. The role of social workers has been to assist the disabled person to cope better with their disability by helping them make personal adjustments and to deal with issues of loss. Some commentators have pointed out that social work has emphasised a medical and individualised model of practice in search of professional status as the best way of asserting its expertise (Oliver and Sapey, 2006).

Oliver (1993) outlines the ways in which dependency has been created through service delivery to disabled people. Many services available for disabled people are institutionalised, with rigid routine activities that largely fail to involve disabled people in day-to-day operations and overall policy. This situation creates dependency as power and control remain firmly in the hands of professional staff. Oliver (1993, p 54) points out that "disabled people are offered little choice about aids and equipment, times at which professionals can attend to help with matters like toileting, dressing or preparing a meal are restricted, and the limited range of tasks that professionals can perform are further limited because of professional boundaries, employer requirements or trade union practices".

The condition of dependency is also found in the professional–client relationship associated with issues of unequal power. Even though the language of 'client' has been changed to 'user' or 'consumer' the controlling functions of social workers still exist. Oliver (1993) suggests one of the ways to change a dependency-creating relationship to a dependency-reducing one is to expand the notion of independence from physical achievements to planning and creating services in partnership with disabled people.

The medical model has had a profound impact on the lives of disabled people, not least because this individualised approach undermines the possibility of recognising disabled people as a social group who share experiences of stigma, exclusion, discrimination and forced dependency. Swain et al (2005, p 23) points out that:

> ... the medical model is reinforced through wider cultural representation of disability and disabled people.... The unquestioned assumption that disabled people have extra or 'special' needs for care, support and help is used to legitimize the separate provision of services in areas such as education, housing, public transport, training and employment.

The medical model pays little attention to societal attitudes, barriers and environments that have limited opportunities for people with disabilities to participate fully in society. The controlling aspects of social work compounded the barriers and limitations already in place to keep disabled people in a dependent position in society.

This model of disability can also affect the way disabled people think about themselves. Clark (2003, p 66) maintains that "many disabled people internalise the negative message that all disabled people's problems stem from not having 'normal' bodies. Disabled people too can be led to believe that their impairments automatically prevent them participating in social activities". By internalising these negative messages, disabled people are less likely to challenge their exclusion from mainstream society (Clark, 2003). The adverse implications of the medical model have led to the adoption of a social model of disability; however, many aspects of the medical model remain tied to social work theory and practice.

A social model of disability

The disability movement has been successful in challenging the medical model of disability, highlighting its oppressive features and adverse impact on the lives of disabled people. The social model developed by disabled people themselves places the definition of disability firmly in a social context. The social model of disability recognises that disability is socially created and is detrimental to individuals who experience sensory and physical impairments. Thus a distinction is made between impairment and disability. Disability is seen as the combination of social, physical and attitudinal barriers. This is because society disables people who have impairments by preventing their full participation in social life. In this way, for disabled people to be included in everyday life, barriers must be removed to bring about social change.

Some of these barriers are:

- institutional discrimination
- stereotypes and negative attitudes
- inflexible organisational practices and procedures
- inaccessible buildings and transport.

One of the best illustrations of a social model of disability is drawn from a study by Groce (1988), cited in Oliver (1996), called *Everyone here spoke sign language*. The study focused on a small and isolated North American community known as Martha's Vineyard. What is distinctive about this community is the fact that there is a very high incidence of profound hereditary deafness and that all community members are bilingual. The two languages used by members of this bilingual community are English and sign language. During an interview with a hearing woman a question was asked about hearing-impaired members of her community whom the researcher described as handicapped. The respondent said "those people weren't handicapped they were just deaf". So clearly, in Martha's Vineyard, hearing impairment is not a disability, it is simply a normal variation that people expect to find and that the social environment has evolved to encompass.

Following this example, the social model of disability locates the causes of disability in the physical and social environment rather than with the individual. This approach views individuals as not possessing a disability but an impairment that means that people who are in some way physically or mentally different from other people may have all kinds of potential skills and abilities. These potential skills are often ignored or undermined by the majority because of their unwillingness to embrace diversity so in effect such people are disabled by the social and physical environment in which they live. In the social model of disability, society is seen as having a responsibility to adapt to and accommodate the needs of people who have impairments. Ahmad (2000, p 1) explores this point further: "the fundamental argument is that the disability resides in the workings of an unjust society; a more inclusive environment ranging from inclusive employment, education and transport policies would allow people with impairments to perform their roles as citizens".

A social model of disability is closely aligned with the development of disability movements and disabled service users. The disabled people's movement is one of the most established and visible movements to challenge social policy and social work as well as public consciousness about issues of disability. This challenge demanded dominant understanding about disability to be reframed in terms of rights and anti-discrimination coupled with the idea of independent living. Disabled people have organised around local and national groups and developed their own ways of working by putting forward their direct experience of policies and services they have received. As these developments unfolded it became clear that disabled people would no longer accept social exclusion and mechanisms of oppression set up within services that were designed to cater for their needs.

Despite the positive elements of a social model of disability, several commentators have raised concerns that this model has a tendency to deny the individual experience of impairment. This means that there is a danger here of presenting issues of disability in a simple way so that individuals' experiences of impairment are sidelined or ignored. For some disabled people, the onset of impairment is a personal tragedy that includes emotional dimensions to this experience.

Black disabled people and a social model of disability

Black disabled commentators have put forward another criticism of this model. Stuart (1996) suggests that although the social model has been important in understanding the collective discrimination and exclusion of disabled people, this model tends to present disabled people as a homogeneous group. This frame of reference fails to take into account differences among disabled people and the social realities of multiple oppressions. Many black disabled people say that racism operates within the disability movement in the same way as in other organisations and institutions in British society.

Disability organisations are not immune from racism or operating in oppressive ways and this may be one of the reasons for the absence of black people in many mainstream voluntary and disability groups (Oliver and Sapey, 2006). These concerns have been difficult to accept by disability groups. In many ways this position parallels the feminist movement when black women articulated criticism of racism among white women. Black women directed attention to the differences and intensity of discrimination among women. As Carby (1982) points out, black women are subject to simultaneous forms of oppression such as patriarchy, race and class.

Developments in understanding the interrelatedness of discriminations have called into question the 'double jeopardy' or 'double discrimination' perspective in describing the experiences of black disabled people. One of the problems with this approach is that 'double jeopardy' tends to present discrimination as separate features of existence. Even though double jeopardy describes the way oppressions add up over time and in their intensity, this approach misses the social-structural connection between them (Andersen and Hill-Collins, 2004).

Stuart (1993) also rejects this approach as being inadequate to challenge oppressive models of disability and the experience of black disabled people as British citizens. By highlighting the social realities of black disabled people it becomes apparent that although the common features of race, gender and disability discrimination have their unique characteristics, they are also interrelated. Following these concerns, double jeopardy perspectives have been replaced by a more sophisticated understanding of interlocking discrimination or systems of oppression to describe the complex nature of discrimination that contributes significantly to the precarious situation of disabled black people. A black disabled woman makes known the social realities of being located within a separate or single source of oppression:

> ... as a black woman, I can't say well I'll deal with my gender today and 'my race' tomorrow, because I have to deal with it as one person, you know. And the same can be said of disabled people and lesbians and gays, black disabled people; you know whatever combination of oppression that you may say. (Evans and Banton, 2000, p 47)

Valuing personal experiences is significant for people whose experiences and lives are not reflected in mainstream society and can act as a vehicle for empowerment. According to Stuart (2006, p 173), although there is some similarity between the experience of black people and disabled people, the literature often fails to represent this. He explains that "although many writers on disability acknowledge that disability is a social construction, that disability is 'created' by society; there is a great deal of reluctance to discuss 'race' fully within the context of disability".

Black disabled people sometimes find themselves alienated from disability groups that by their very nature are organised solely around disability. As a result of this approach, they tend to sideline issues of race and gender, and black disabled people are in effect encouraged to prioritise disability at the expense of their identities as black people. Stuart (1993, p 99) suggests that the starting point for black disabled people should be to address their marginalisation:

> ... unlike other sections of society in a similar situation, black people are systematically portrayed as outsiders and interlopers. This analysis creates a clear separation between the relative experience of black and white disabled people. It reinforces my belief that being a black disabled person is not a 'double' experience, but a single one grounded in British racism.

In a study by Evans and Banton (2000), black disabled people felt that agencies often failed to recognise the impact of multiple oppression that left black disabled people unsure of where to turn. Participants in the study felt that there was stigma attached to disability in some black communities and one of the contributing factors to this situation was the lack of awareness-raising work on disability.

Independent living and direct payments

The notion of independence and personal autonomy are highly valued in western societies and are generally considered to be something that most people should desire and strive for. For most disabled people, independent living is seen as an important goal that will enable them to live a better quality of life. Historically, disabled people have been seen as dependent, requiring constant care and attention. Their exclusion from the workforce also compounds social and economic dependency. This situation has been reinforced by welfare professionals through adopting a medical or individualised approach to practice that encourages dependency and control of disabled people's lives. In this context, independent living has been advanced as the best way to support disabled people and improve their quality of life.

For some black disabled people, the notion of independence seems to undermine the importance of families, culture and collective struggles for recognition and presence in their lives. Notwithstanding stigma towards disability in some black communities, families and social networks can offer a buffer in the context of societal racism and neglect (Graham, 2002). In this way, many black people highly value interdependency as a cultural norm but at the same time want 'independent' living in a more considered way.

The introduction of direct payments (cash in lieu of social services) has been a significant step forward in assisting disabled people to achieve independent living. This social policy supports a social model of disability. Unlike other forms of support, direct payments are given to disabled people to provide an opportunity for them to purchase services and to have control over their everyday lives.

During the 1980s, direct payment schemes were first introduced in limited areas of the UK. Many local authorities were reluctant to initiate direct payment schemes because they considered them to be too risky and they were sceptical about implementation (Swain et al, 2004). Direct payments are seen as one of the ways to ensure equality for disabled people. The widespread introduction of direct payments through the 1996 Community Care (Direct Payments) Act allowed disabled people to have choice and control. As Hasler (2004, p 221) maintains:

> Direct payments matter [for individual users] because they give them choice and control. They can arrange services from a person they choose, at times they choose, for assistance delivered in a way they control. Disabled people

interviewed about the benefits of direct payments say things like, 'Its given me my life back' or 'I've got my freedom'.... Direct payments [enable] users to get more than a choice of bedtimes. The flexibility offered by the system allows people to work, to travel, to be active parents, in short to do the range of things that non-disabled people expect to do.

Stuart (2005, p 55) examined direct payment schemes to understand how this strategy could be utilised more fully by black disabled people, and reported that service users from black communities face considerable barriers. Here are some of the barriers identified:

- misunderstanding about the meaning of 'independent living';
- inadequate assessments that give little attention to the background to service users and their specific need;
- a lack of appropriate information about the direct payments scheme;
- a shortage of appropriate advocacy and support services;
- possible confusion over the direct payments rules concerning close relatives;
- difficulties in recruiting personal assistants able to meet the cultural, linguistic and religious requirements for service users (adapted from Stuart, 2005, p 55).

There is evidence that black people receive poorer services overall from local authorities and Stuart (2005) suggests that the low take-up of the direct payments scheme is indicative of the general lack of attention to the welfare of black service users. One of the difficulties in implementing this scheme is that it is still dependent to some extent on the discretion of care managers that may determine whether or not black disabled people use the direct payments scheme. Following these concerns, some black disabled people are wary of the autonomous lifestyle that independent living seems to advocate. This may be an important factor in the low take-up of direct payments among service users from black communities. Stuart (2005, p 62) makes the point that:

> ... the key philosophy behind direct payments is that they should increase the independence of disabled people for whom receiving services from providers has always meant a lack of choice and a loss of independence. However, this is a Eurocentric interpretation of independence, where

disabled people make decisions independently of carers and family.

Another issue that emerges is the shortage of appropriate advocacy and support services for black disabled people. In the past, many voluntary organisations ignored the views and concerns of black disabled people, even when organisations were run by disabled people themselves. Similarly, black organisations sometimes neglect the complex situation of being black and disabled (Stuart, 1996). These experiences of marginalisation have contributed to gaps in support and service users from black communities remain poorly served. In relation to these gaps in support, most young black disabled people want opportunities to meet other young people who share similar food and a way of life and to learn about their culture and to socialise and share experiences. Although aspects of independent living and direct payments are problematic for some black disabled service users, there are examples of successful support services and practice that engage service users in the development of such services.

Conclusion

This chapter has looked at several issues concerning disability and black communities. The chapter started by considering definitions of disability and the way they have shaped social policy and models of social work with disabled people. Legislative reforms have been slow to address entrenched inequalities and discrimination against disabled people to bring about civil rights and a better quality of life. Social work practice with disabled people was influenced by the medical model and this frame of reference encouraged paternalism and dependency. Another model in which disability could be understood is the moral model of disability that tended to view disabled people as in perpetual need of charity and care.

The social model of disability has gained influence and has been adopted as the best way to work with disabled people because of its focus on social barriers, attitudes and institutions in society and the part they play in creating disadvantage and discrimination. Even though this model of disability has been useful in highlighting discrimination and spearheading new ways of understanding disability based on disabled people's knowledge and experience, there are differences between disabled people, and some black disabled people have felt marginalised and sometimes excluded.

The starting point for understanding the experiences of black disabled people has taken the form of double jeopardy, but this interpretation has been rejected by many black disabled people because it separates categories of experience in a way that seems to do little to challenge existing inequalities. A more sophisticated understanding of the experiences of black disabled people has been drawn from thinking about the relationships between disability and race and linking them together. Here, this more inclusive framework can produce experiences and knowledge of social realities to decrease marginalisation and exclusion.

Another issue dealt with in this chapter is independent living and direct payments that are seen as a significant step forward in promoting a better quality of life for disabled people. Overall, these new initiatives have been welcomed by some black communities but there are issues concerning the meanings of independent living and the possibility of undermining family ties. There also appears to be some concern about direct payments and this is reflected in the low take-up of direct payments among black disabled people. There is much work to do in social work practice to meet the needs and aspirations of black disabled people. Recent research has highlighted the experiences of black disabled people and what is needed now is action and change.

SEVEN

Ageing

Introduction

In recent years social work with older people has become a more important area of practice. As more people are now living longer into old age, social workers are likely to work with older people who experience dementia and ill health, and those in greatest need. In these situations, social workers deal with complex needs bearing in mind the need to assist older people in maintaining their independence with the help of packages of social care and support.

There is general agreement that improvements in public health, housing, food supplies, working conditions and medical advances have contributed to increased average life expectancy. These gains indicate the way in which social policy directly affects the experience of old age. Although many older people remain in good health, the level of retirement pensions and provision of health and social care are also important factors in the overall experience of old age. Some older people have accumulated occupational pensions, private savings and purchased their own homes, while others find themselves dependent on state pensions for their incomes and on declining public welfare services.

In many respects understanding patterns of inequality in society over the lifespan can shed light on the range of different individual experiences in old age. For example, long-standing inequalities experienced by women in the labour market, combined with disadvantages in social security policy, are carried into old age so that the risk of poverty increases. It is also widely recognised that social divisions become more apparent in later stages of life as inequalities of gender, race and disability become more critical in shaping people's lives. Women are in the majority in later life and some authors have described old age as the world of women. The increased longevity of women contributes to their likelihood of living alone and experiencing long-term disabling conditions (Phillips et al, 2006). Growing poverty among older women has drawn the attention of sociologists and they have used the term the 'feminisation' of poverty to describe these new patterns of poverty among women and particularly older women.

Generally, older women have a lower level of private pensions because of interrupted and part-time employment careers to take care of their families (Ginn, 2003).

Older people from black communities also experience patterns of inequality over the lifespan. Although there are wide variations of income across black communities, black people are more likely to work in lower paid jobs that do not attract occupational pension schemes. This situation is sometimes exacerbated by insufficient National Insurance contributions to qualify for a full pension (Berthoud, 2002). Even though people are living longer, there are uneven patterns of longevity by ethnicity as well as gender. Among black populations, there are high incidences of ill health including higher rates of coronary heart disease for people of Pakistani and Bangladeshi origin. Higher levels of hypertension among Caribbean populations and a higher incidence of diabetes for all black communities are also reported (Modood et al, 1997).

In reviewing these developments, this chapter opens by looking at the background and context of current issues in social policy and ageing with particular reference to black older people. The next section reviews social divisions in old age and then moves on to look at the complexities of migration and growing old outside their country of origin. By applying current models of ageing to older people from black communities, new initiatives can emerge that take account of different circumstances and concerns. Finally, there is a brief consideration of life history research and oral history as an important approach to understanding ageing from black perspectives.

Background and context – policy responses to ageing

Many commentators have used the term 'an ageing world' or 'global greying' to describe the shift in the composition of populations in western societies. The 'baby boomer' (a phrase coined for the large number of people born between 1947 and 1964) generation are now reaching retirement age and attracting attention in social policy with concerns about the projected increase in the number of people eligible for state pensions. Can society afford to pay for the cost of pensions in the light of welfare spending constraints? What kinds of services will be needed? These questions have taken centre stage in public discussions about the 'burden' of older people in health and social welfare spending and the need for people to make individual plans early in their work career for retirement. As these discussions have become more prevalent with images of an impending 'welfare crisis', old age has taken on a social problem perspective that is not new and underlies many concerns about this time of life (Victor, 2005).

Social workers will need to have a wider understanding of the ageing process to practise successfully. This entails rethinking conventional models of ageing that feature decline, dysfunction and disengagement rather than viewing old age in a positive way. In a society where youth is highly valued, old age is often seen in a negative light. Discrimination against older people known as ageism has become more prevalent in recent years and social work needs to adopt a critical understanding of old age to assist practitioners to work in an effective way.

In order to understand more about ageing, social work draws on the discipline of gerontology that describes a broad area of study about the ageing process and includes biological, psychological and social perspectives. Gerontology holds a multidisciplinary frame of reference and has been influential in shaping social work practice with older people. Recently, gerontology has largely focused on old age as a distinct phase of life in the life cycle when older people disengage from social life to take up new roles or activities. It is claimed that this transition away from society allows for the smooth transition of social power across generations. Several authors have pointed out that this theory has had a negative impact on older people generally because it has informed much of health and social care policy (Estes, 2001; Victor, 2005). Moreover, these early theories in gerontology reveal little discussion or concern about the linkages between ageing and patterns of inequality and the differences between older people. In the current climate a great deal of research literature has produced a critical approach to gerontology dealing with issues of gender, race and class as well as questioning commonly held views about ageing in society (Wilson, 2000; Estes et al, 2003).

As people are healthier than those in past generations, many older people can expect to remain active and productive throughout their lives. This means that ageing is not necessarily a period of sharp decline and dependency but instead many of the processes of ageing can be delayed or modified through medical advances and a healthy lifestyle. Successful ageing has developed as a positive approach to growing old by promoting steps that individuals can take to proactively prevent decline and adapt to changes that may occur. This model of ageing has been popular in social care because its focus on independent living and a healthy lifestyle resonates with current social work practice with older people.

While at the outset successful ageing appears to offer a more positive understanding of ageing, its individualised strategies have been criticised for failing to tackle inequalities and discrimination that are closely associated with ageing. The experience of old age is both the same and different for men and women, black and disabled people as well as different experiences between individuals at different periods of their 'old age'. Just as the experiences and situation of women in old age are socially conditioned, the lived experiences of black older people are marked by their disadvantaged social, political and economic status in society.

Gerontology has neglected issues of migration in later life or growing old in a foreign country, which are important features of many black older people's lives. The commonly held view that black families will 'look after their own' still remains and this stereotype often masks the real needs of this group of older people. It is only fairly recently that the views, needs and aspirations of black older people are being considered in terms of changes needed in policy, planning and service delivery. Although there has been an upsurge in research in recent years, many black older people expressed concern about being 'over-researched' and research that seemed to be taking place for its own sake rather than as a springboard for action and social change in design or service delivery (Butt and O'Neil, 2004).

In a similar way there has been little attention paid to the way changes in community care might affect black communities. Again, as mentioned in Chapter Six on disability, a model of double jeopardy, or for black women triple jeopardy, has been a popular way of describing the experiences of ageism, racism and sexism in relation to structural disadvantages that place black older people in a precarious position. Although jeopardy theories highlight the issues of oppression and disadvantage, they are weak in giving voice to black older people themselves and listening to their experiences and needs.

Many authors have recounted a history of neglect in adult services leading to the development of unsatisfactory institutional provision and inadequate community-based support services (Baldock, 1993; Phillips et al, 2006). Early studies about older people can be found in research looking at poverty in the general population. For example, during the 19th century Booth's study of poverty in London (1892, 1894) revealed a graphic description of poverty among older people at a higher level than the general population and resulted in the introduction of minimal pensions to some older people to deal with basic needs. From these early poverty studies it is clear that there is a close association between poverty and age.

Postwar developments put in place comprehensive welfare services with plans to provide welfare from 'the cradle to the grave'. The introduction of universal healthcare and social services provided no specific services for older people per se but brought major improvements in health across the lifespan into old age. Pensions were also introduced based on subsistence levels that were barely adequate but in line with social security policies that directed benefits to be kept below wage levels.

Several authors have accounted for these developments. Alcock (1993, p 173) points out that one of the reasons for the low level of basic pensions is that it "acts as an important incentive for employed people to seek additional private financial protection for their old age". As many older people depend on pensions as their sole income, it is not surprising that the low level of pensions pushes older people into poverty. This is particularly the case for vulnerable populations where inequalities during working life influence the life cycle and experiences of old age.

Beyond this situation, as older people move into deep old age and savings may have been depleted, circumstances tend to deteriorate and experiences of deprivation become more acute. Alcock (1993) argues that because policy developments about retirement are based on assumptions associated with chronological age it is assumed that older people can no longer contribute and become a burden to society. In this way, social constructions of old age are foisted on older people so that social policies operate both to create and reproduce poverty and dependency.

For older people in greatest need, the 1948 National Assistance Act placed a duty on local authorities to provide residential care. Over time, institutional care for older people has been heavily criticised with particular concerns about standards of nursing and social care. Institutional care was often of poor quality and older people lived in isolation, segregated from communities. These critiques about institutional care generally led to a rethinking about services and growing demands for community-based planning for older people, with residential care for those where no other alternatives would meet their complex needs. This shift was strengthened by political changes and the rise of the 'New Right' that reflected the government's reluctance to make resources available to vulnerable groups in society.

With the introduction of the 1990 NHS and Community Care Act, a framework for reorganising social services along market principles marked a change in the way social services were delivered. Local authorities were encouraged to embrace market principles to enable private enterprise and voluntary agencies to act as providers of care. The Act required local authorities to make arrangements to purchase services from these agencies as well as provide in-house care services. The framework created a mixed economy of provision and a contract culture developed in which social services were involved in purchasing the majority of services. This framework was intended to give choice to older people about the services they receive with an emphasis on assessing needs and care planning.

Another feature of the Act was the right to a community care assessment that would form the basis of a needs-led tailor-made package of social care. However, despite the reorganisation of social services and ideals of community-based care, these developments were built on the state providing minimal care that would be supplemented by families and the independent sector. In effect, this legislation promoted minimal services for those in greatest need, providing domiciliary services such as home care, lunch clubs, Meals on Wheels, aids and adaptations to the home and day centres. These home care services would be provided until it was deemed that an older person developed a more complex level of needs that required admission to residential or nursing home care. This model of care in the community appears to reflect models of ageing prevalent in the wider society where decline and dependency are established as the norm with little attention paid to rehabilitation and the creation of supportive environments (Ray and Phillips, 2002).

Since these reforms, community-based care has become a key social policy objective in supporting and caring for older people. Recent policy developments have considered the views and wishes of older people themselves rather than expecting older people to fit into services already provided. Following New Labour's modernising social services agenda, services for older people have come under scrutiny in efforts to standardise services and strengthen an integrated multiagency approach to ensure equitable treatment and promote quality of life issues. The changing role of social workers to care managers affected social work practice that required practical skills as well as 'people' skills, taking time to communicate and offer support. Given this context, it was recognised that joint working within a multidisciplinary team can promote a more holistic approach to meeting needs.

In the social care field, there were no national standards to ensure quality and a range of services across the country that led to variations in access to care, quality of care and care outcomes (Victor, 2005). Under the *National Service Framework for older people* (DH, 2001b), targets were set out with an emphasis on person-centred care, prevention and multiagency working. One of the features of this framework is that it addresses age discrimination by making it clear that NHS services should be based on clinical need and preventing social services departments from using age in their eligibility criteria to restrict access to services (McDonald, 2006). Another important feature of this framework relates to black older people and recognition of their particular needs.

National Service Framework for older people: key themes

- Respecting individuals.
- Providing person-centred care.
- Rooting out age discrimination.
- Intermediate care and rehabilitation.
- Fitting services around people's needs.
- Recognition of particular needs of older people from black and ethnic minorities.
- Promotion of health and active life in older age.

Source: DH (2001b)

Black people and ageing

Older people from black and minority ethnic communities are a small but growing population. The population of black older people has risen rapidly in recent years from 61,000 in 1981, to 350,000 in 2001 (ONS, 2003). Groups of older people who migrated to Britain in the 1950s and 1960s are moving into retirement and old age. This means that black older people are becoming more visible and their presence can no longer be ignored. There is growing concern about the considerable health and social care needs of older people from black communities. With higher rates of unemployment and low levels of income in black communities there is a greater risk of poverty being carried over into old age. Older people in many black communities experience more physical ill health with higher rates of stroke, hypertension, diabetes and heart disease. Although older people from black communities experience similar difficulties as the majority population they also experience stress associated with dealing with racism and a lack of recognition of their cultural heritage.

Community care services continue to be underdeveloped for black service users. There are several reasons for this situation. First, social welfare operates a universal approach to services where it is expected that people will adapt to what is provided rather than developing services around the needs of service users. This 'like it or lump it' attitude is a persistent problem and has resulted in the underuse of social care services by black older people. Added to this approach to services is a tendency to resort to the idea that 'they look after their own'. In certain circumstances, these common myths about family networks have led to the exclusion of black older people from support services they may need. In several research studies black older people reported that they were frustrated by the lack of relevant information about services as well as the lack of appropriate services to meet their needs (Butt, 1994; Rai-Atkins, 2002). Rai-Atkins (2002, p 4) mentions that:

> Black service users and carers in contact with statutory services felt unvalued and misunderstood and usually chose to withdraw from active participation. Those remaining engaged with mainstream services often felt they found themselves amidst a patronising environment and shaped by stereotypical attitudes.

Access to mainstream services remains problematic for many black older people with particular concerns about language barriers and the attitudes of service providers. Although there has been more attention paid to the needs and aspirations of black service users, the tension between developments of specific services or making changes and strengthening mainstream services remains. Some professionals agree that both approaches are needed to ensure equitable and better quality services leading to better outcomes.

Second, the recent policy changes that encourage service users' participation have tended to ignore or marginalise the needs of black service users. It is also claimed that black service users may be further disadvantaged because community care tends to individualise problems and service arrangements are based on white norms (Cameron et al, 1996). There is a long way to go to make sure black service users are heard and that their views count in the development of appropriate services.

Third, as noted earlier in this chapter, recent changes in the way services are delivered have resulted in voluntary organisations playing a significant role in providing services. Many black voluntary organisations developed as a result of service users being excluded and receiving a poor service from mainstream organisations. It is often the case that funding favours large well-established voluntary organisations even though small organisations offer services that people want and benefit communities in various ways. Black voluntary organisations offer a range of services that include education and training, health support, welfare and legal advice, advocacy, day care facilities, cultural activities, housing and accommodation. Historically, black voluntary organisations have been poorly funded, often overstretched and marginal to local policy debates. In a study of 700 and 3,000 'black' non-governmental organisations in Leicester and London respectively, voluntary organisations were seen in a limited capacity as service deliverers and often not involved in local policy-making activities (Chouhan and Lusane, 2004).

Research findings from the Race Equality Unit indicate that service users supported black voluntary organisations and felt that they played a significant role in providing appropriate and supportive services yet these organisations tended to be financially insecure. Despite these disadvantages, a recent survey of voluntary and community organisations indicated that, contrary to popular perceptions, organisations had staying power, with many having been in existence for 10 years or more (McLeod et al, 2001).

Older people from black and minority ethnic groups:

- experience more physical ill health
- are more likely to face poverty
- have poorer access to benefits and pensions
- share experiences of ageism and racism
- need different approaches across different communities.

Source: Butt and O'Neil (2004)

Ageing in a second homeland and issues of migration

Globalisation, better communication and easier travel have opened up more opportunities for some older people. This positive way of thinking about migration does not apply to enforced migration of older people due to war or as victims of disasters. In these circumstances, leaving behind a life in their country of origin presents new challenges as older people face the loss of social networks and many difficulties living in their adopted country.

In British society there is a long tradition of older people moving away from the cities to the countryside or to live by the seaside. In recent years significant numbers of older people are moving to Europe, particularly Spain or France, for their retirement, in search of a better climate and to improve their quality of life. These developments indicate lifestyle choices available to some older people particularly as high property values and occupational pensions have allowed them to purchase lower priced properties abroad. Of course, none of these options are problem free; during the early years of retirement when people are healthy and active this seems a positive way of improving quality of life. However, as older people move into deep old age health and mobility difficulties begin to surface and returning to their country of origin may be a necessary alternative.

Issues of migration are particularly important for older people from black communities. Wilson (2000) maintains that while lifestyle migrants have been the subject of research, older people in different circumstances have been largely ignored. This is the case for black older people. When migrants arrived in Britain in the 1950s and 1960s, the idea of 'going home' to their country of origin was an aspiration that older people wanted to achieve at the end of their working lives. But as they settled and future generations became more established, the prospect of 'going home' became more problematic and was even discarded or more difficult to achieve. Some older people have made creative arrangements that satisfied their need to live in their country of origin and spend significant periods with their families. This solution involves long journeys that can become more difficult as people get older and depends on the financial resources of the younger generation.

Some older people have decided to leave Britain altogether, particularly during the early years of retirement, but this option is not without its difficulties. Sometimes it may be difficult to adjust and make new social networks when returning home; many family members or friends may have passed away and it may be more difficult to blend into communities left many years ago than first realised. Having no choice in the matter and staying put is the social reality for many black older people because their economic circumstances restrict options available to them. Many older people want to stay in Britain to be near their children, particularly black women living on their own. Wilson (2000, p 76) encapsulates the difficulties and complexities of growing old in places where they have spent most of their lives:

> Migration is like a chronic disease. There is no cure ... this negative view highlights the problems that many older migrants face if they try to escape racism in the country of destination and return to their place of origin. They are foreigners in the country of destination but equally when they return to their place of origin they can find themselves as the 'English' ... or some other term implying alienation.

Of course, this is not necessarily the case for all older people returning to their country of origin and sometimes this can be successful and fulfilling for all concerned. However, it is not a straightforward option for many people.

In a research study undertaken by Phillipson and Ahmed (2004, p 164), researchers interviewed older women who had migrated from Bangladesh about support networks and their lives in London's East End. These older women spoke about their life experiences and major changes that have shaped their experiences of ageing.

Migration in later life

"In Bangladesh it would be different. There are lots of people around. I would have my mother-in law and sisters-in-law to help. Everyone would be together. Their uncles could take them to school. I wouldn't have to do that duty." (Khadija, married with four children)

"It is much harder in this country. Here we have to take them to school, bring them home, they need so many things. It was never like this in Bangladesh. In Bangladesh I would have more help. In this country I am on my own. I have to do everything. I have been cleaning the house since this morning. Children in this country aren't very good at cleaning, are they? So I have to do it all myself." (Rafeya, married with five children)

"It would have been harder in Bangladesh. There would be more worries. There is more work to do there. In this country you don't have to worry about harvests and crops, in Bangladesh you do. There is a lot of outdoor work. Here it is all indoors." (Sadika, married with six children) (quoted in Phillipson and Ahmed, 2004, p 164)

The themes discussed in this research study help to bring issues and experiences of migration centre stage in gerontology that tends to assume a linear model and continuity as the basis for ageing studies. To fully understand the experiences of ageing it is necessary to look at issues of migration and their impact on the ageing process. Social work has tended to shy away from issues of migration in later life and their importance in the experience of old age. Unfortunately, issues of entitlement remain embedded in social services and social care and often older people from black communities are unaware of services that may be available to them to decrease social exclusion and improve quality of life.

Models of ageing

Although there have been several models of ageing in recent years, the disengagement theory still dominates much of ageing studies. As the first major model of ageing, disengagement theory generated much discussion and debate for many years. This theory views old age as a distinct phase of life where the individual is engaged in a process of withdrawal from society. Withdrawal starts as people leave their jobs and enter retirement. Following retirement there is a gradual reduction in social activities and social relationships leading to preparation for death. This process of disengagement is viewed as beneficial for both the individual and society because it allows for the smooth transmission of social power from older people to the younger generation.

Many authors argue that this model of ageing has had a negative impact on older people particularly in health and social policies because it seems to encourage indifference to the difficulties of older people and fails to deal with issues of discrimination and social exclusion (Biggs, 2004; Victor, 2005). Victor (2005) maintains that the disengagement model seems to hold a pathway towards successful ageing by reducing social involvement and social interaction. However, as Victor (2005, p 21) points out, "although a negative pathway to the nirvana of successful ageing, it is not conceptually different from other ways to a successful old age such as dietary adaptations (such as eating yoghurt) or religious or physical activity".

Ageing and the life course

Life course perspectives hold chronological age as the basis for social roles that are shaped by the norms associated with particular age groups. In every society there are norms tied to a particular phase of life and these norms are shared by groups in society. The notion of the life course is a powerful way of framing old age as people journey through life. Although life course/stage models have been widely accepted in social work, they have become less popular over time because this perspective pays little attention to issues of power and factors such as gender, ethnicity and class that shape experiences of ageing. The absence of these factors in understanding old age are highly relevant for social work because this model tends to cast the difficulties of older people as personal failures and a lack of responsibility.

A further issue that emerges is that the boundaries between life stages are weakening as more people move away from age norms and associated social roles. For example, the age of retirement is changing with people retiring over extended periods, therefore, the linkages between old age and retirement become more blurred and difficult to define (Andersson and Oberg, 2004). Another example that has a bearing on this issue is that some women become grandmothers in their forties and fifties, yet many women do not see themselves as old and reject traditional images of grandmothers and some of the associated social role expectations.

For black older people, issues of migration are important factors in their life course and it is often assumed that older people will find it more difficult to adjust; this therefore changes the experience of old age particularly as the migrant's life course is interrupted by migration. Although life course perspectives tend to provide an explanation of the social obligations that are assigned to each phase of life, this approach takes no account of how the boundaries of stages are defined and when a person enters and leaves a particular stage in life.

Successful ageing

Although successful or positive ageing has assumed greater prominence in recent years, particularly among the helping professions, there is little agreement about what it means to age well. For some commentators, positive ageing is about being productive and life satisfaction while for others it means to cope with changes and the capacity for self-care and maintaining a positive outlook. Policy makers have been enthusiastic about this approach and have identified three key areas as vehicles for social change:

- raise the expectations of older people and avoid making judgements on age but rather on their 'true' value;
- encourage older people – 50 plus – to stay in work;
- remove incentives to retire early and increase volunteering for people in retirement (Cabinet Office, 2000).

As Biggs (2004) maintains, developments in policy have attempted to turn common perceptions about the burden of old age into an opportunity. Positive ageing replaces views of old age as one of dependency and decline with encouraging active and healthy lifestyles, changes in behaviour, eating a balanced diet and regular exercise. It is suggested that as people get older they tend to drop goals and activities, but successful ageing encourages a positive attitude and a rekindling of goals that fit with an individual's situation and circumstances. Instead of thinking about ageing as a downward path, it is important to be positive and adjust to changes that may occur.

Moody (2001) is sceptical of this approach because it is seen to operate a remedial intervention perspective that divides older people into the 'welderly and the illderly' so that successful ageing is about survival. Older people are encouraged to maintain their own ageing process by incorporating individual strategies to delay or work with changes, in other words adjust to changes that occur. Successful ageing assumes a homogeneous society and does not seem to acknowledge inequalities as people enter old age.

In a qualitative study of older people from Iran living in a second homeland of Sweden, Torres (2004) reports that migrants claimed that an Iranian approach to ageing equates to becoming more dignified and this characteristic equated to conventions for how old people should behave. Many older people described the features of successful ageing in this way:

> A busy schedule and a future-orientated outlook in old age are apparently not really appropriate ways to tackle the later stages of life. To age successfully in Iran is therefore the same as slowing down and living a much quieter, disengaged and passive life than that lived as a younger adult. (Torres, 2004, p 131)

Some older people were quite surprised to find that older people in the host community continued to look forward and make plans whereas successful ageing in their country of origin associated successful ageing with dependency on their children. Torres (2004) suggests that successful ageing and its links to personal autonomy changed the way ageing was considered but there were variations about ideas of ageing well both in their country of origin and second homeland. However, older people did not expect their children who had been socialised in Sweden to look after them as they moved into old age and this study suggested a weakening of family obligations.

Ageing in different cultures

So far in this chapter, dominant perceptions of old age as a time of dependency and physical decline have been outlined. These generalised beliefs emerged from scientific approaches that have increased our knowledge and understanding of the human body and the ageing process. However, people age differently, and therefore it is difficult to connect chronological age exactly with many aspects of the human body. For example, many people in their seventies are healthy, fit and active while others have long-term disabilities or chronic illnesses (Wilson, 2000). These facets of the ageing process influence ideas about old age in society generally and shape the experiences of older people.

Bearing this in mind, culture plays a significant role in understanding what it means to be old in contemporary society. As the older population is becoming more diverse, older people pass through later life with different worldviews and values that shape their experiences of ageing (Wilson, 2000). Many cultures across the world consider old age in different ways. It is difficult to explore these understandings of old age in a general way without a tendency of creating or reproducing stereotypes that may already be widely held in society. However, all societies attach significance to various stages of the life cycle. Older people are often expected to fulfil age-related expectations, social roles and obligations. On the other hand, families and particularly their children are expected to care for their parents in their old age. Older people are expected to be less active and become more content and serene. However, the widely held belief that black families and minorities 'look after their own' has been used to ignore the needs of black older people or to show indifference to their difficulties. These assumptions about the care of ageing parents are often placed within the context of the general practice in majority communities of placing older people in residential homes. In the past cultural traditions have often been viewed as morally superior to the materialistic character of modern society where older people tend to be institutionalised. However, older people were not always supported in traditional societies.

Models of ageing

Disengagement theories
Dependency and decline

↓

Successful/positive ageing
Active and healthy lifestyles

↓

Life course
Age norms and social roles
Cultural themes
Spiritual dimension to ageing

Clearly, some of the traditional structures and norms have weakened and family structures are changing. Although black families are more likely to care for their older relatives at home for longer prior to nursing home admission, families are sometimes unable to provide the care needed for their ageing parents or family members. Not only is housing availability for extended families inadequate in British society but also younger generations have been socialised into a British way of life that tends to encourage personal autonomy, independent living and individualism. Against this background, extended families living together are viewed as outside the 'norm' in British society and in many ways are unsupported in universal policy-making frameworks. Equally important, the assumption that black people live in extended families is simplistic in contemporary British society, as significant numbers of black people live alone or with few relatives in this country (Ahmad, 1996).

Despite the weakening of family structures, cultural factors still influence understanding about old age. These ideas vary across and within cultures and are often more complex than first appears. For example, within African-centred worldviews ideas about ageing are firmly placed within a cultural context that also transcend into a spiritual plane. This spiritual context is dictated by an individual's status within a community. Ageing is viewed as part of the life cycle that usually confers respectability and obligations to pass cultural and life knowledge on to future generations.

However, according to these beliefs, the development of self- or personhood is characterised as an act of becoming through a process of moral growth and development. Personhood is not simply achieved by existence, in other words chronological age, but instead relates to an individual's contribution (or service) to the community. This model rejects a life journey that is linear and marked with decline but instead views life as following the same path as the cosmos – a zigzag spiral pathway. Oba T'Shaka (1995) explains this further:

> The progression of consciousness ... occurs because, as we go through the cycles of life, as we learn the lessons of Maat, the lessons of the cosmos. As we internalize these lessons, we transform our thoughts, words and actions to conform to Maat. We ascend the spiral ladder of transformation through the cycles of life, rising to the level of perfection where the body becomes one with the soul. (T'Shaka, 1995, p 19)

Older people are believed to have wisdom that can be passed on to the next generation. They are often called on to lead or mediate community activities and issues. It is believed that elders hold knowledge, stories and memories about life. This knowledge is contained in many social practices that define the relationship between people and their environment.

In drawing together models of ageing, social work has been heavily influenced by models of ageing that view ageing as a period of decline. In the current climate, successful or positive ageing has been adopted as the way forward to change social attitudes towards ageing and to create positive social work practice with older people, taking into account their diverse range of needs. Cultural understanding of old age needs to be integrated into models of ageing and a recognition that definitions of 'positive' may not be so 'positive' for older people from various communities.

Life histories

In order to appreciate the diversity of ageing and to bring about a more inclusive picture, the experiences of black elders can engage not only personal lived experiences, but also families and sociocultural practices. Hill-Collins (1989) has designed a framework that views black women as 'outsiders', that is, marginalised in the wider society, but they are also 'insiders' because they have a particular viewpoint on self, family and society. This viewpoint includes lived experiences and knowledge about everyday life and how to get through and into the world that has been suppressed and ignored generally, yet these concrete experiences have stimulated a distinct black and female consciousness. In black communities, great value is placed on this knowledge that includes proverbs, stories, riddles, songs and first-hand accounts of living histories as a testament to the human condition in the face of oppression.

As the interest in everyday life, personal accounts and experiences has developed, researchers have turned to life history, biographical interviewing and reminiscence work to understand ageing and to support people in later life. Life history work and oral history continue to play a significant role in uncovering hidden histories and experiences in black communities. Indeed, oral history is a vital research tool in black studies, as Turner (2006, p 330) points out:

> ... oral history empowers people who have been hidden from history by giving them voices to tell their stories and provide firsthand accounts about the recent past, providing pertinent information about the unique experiences of individuals, families, and communities, across localities, cultures, and nationalities ... it saves the memories of our elders and ordinary people whose histories are often neglected and whose records are not preserved in archives and other repositories.

Personal biographies and documents have played a pivotal role in uncovering histories of enslavement and the lives of enslaved peoples throughout the diaspora. Equally important are recent histories of colonial experiences and the impact of these experiences on contemporary life. Black researchers and others have recognised that they need to bring forward the richness of black histories in communities to preserve them for future generations and to bring appreciation to these narratives in the wider society. Many black researchers have adopted oral history as a way of documenting social changes and cultural knowledge, health issues and understandings about life and relationships from the vantage point of lived experiences and 'wisdom' from black elders.

Reminiscence work has developed in social work to support and enable older people to establish meaning in their lives. In addition, this work has also focused on dealing with loss and grief. Some of the rationale for reminiscence work comes from Erikson's theory that individuals pass through a series of developmental stages in life, and part of the ageing process involves a review of life as coming to terms with mistakes, failures and lost opportunities. However, in a climate where positive ageing is promoted, reminiscence work is often viewed as empowering, but Coleman (1974) suggests that there might be three perspectives in reminiscence work:

- reminiscence work that recalls the past and provides a source of strength and self-esteem;
- informative reminiscence work that recalls the past as a way to pass on knowledge;
- life history review that looks at memories of an individual's life to integrate an image of oneself in the face of death.

These perspectives indicate that reminiscence work can bring about positive experiences for older people and their families but can also lead to complex results that are not anticipated. This is particularly important for older people from black communities where experiences of enforced migration as a result of war or disasters bring painful memories and may not be a welcome mental activity (Bornat, 1998).

Conclusion

This chapter has tackled a range of issues concerning older people from black communities. There are several key factors that shape their experiences of ageing. Persistent social inequalities in the labour market and histories of unemployment, together with inequalities in social welfare and health, are carried over into old age and contribute to a greater risk of poverty and social exclusion. The health status of black older people is a cause for concern. There are high rates of heart disease, diabetes and stroke among black older people, yet they are less likely to gain access to health services and there are reports of the worst health outcomes. The new National Service Framework for services for older people is a welcome strategy to set out standards of care and direct payments schemes to promote independent living.

However, assumptions associated with positive ageing may not be so 'positive' for many black older people. There is no single perspective that can adequately explain the experiences of old age and ageing studies has largely ignored their experiences of ageing. Black researchers have been involved in bringing their needs and concerns to the attention of policy makers and canvassing their views and perspectives about their quality of life in Britain today. Unfortunately, the myths surrounding black families that 'they look after their own' have allowed policy makers to ignore or show an indifference to the needs of black older people.

With younger generations sometimes under pressure in contemporary Britain, the unspoken agreements about who will look after their parents should they need care appear to be dwindling. Richards (2006) reports that older black British families of African Caribbean heritage have taken on a British way of life that has served to undermine their family structures and communities. Similar concerns have been voiced throughout Asian communities and black older people are becoming more visible in residential care. Although religion as an important aspect of older people's lives was not explored, these institutions often provide support, social networks and social care.

Despite the social changes in family structures and communities, cultural knowledge remains the lynchpin that shapes worldviews and identities. There are many ongoing discussions about cultural and social practices that seem unreasonable in contemporary Britain, but younger generations want to retain empowering features of their cultural heritage that provide a culturally holding environment for many people.

EIGHT

Concluding comments

In the past social work tended to marginalise or exclude perspectives from different vantage points in favour of conventional or mainstream thinking about social life. As the limitations of class analysis became recognised, other forms of oppression such as sexism and racism as the experiences of communities and groups surfaced into the public arena. However, just as feminist theories and practice tended to be neglected in social science generally, black perspectives have remained largely on the outer edges of research agendas and interest. Nevertheless, there has been a steady growth of black scholars who are seeking to influence social work practice and make visible marginalised interpretations of social life, and particularly black service users.

Although social work has long produced a flurry of literature addressing issues of equality, diversity and social justice in both theory and practice, these values and priorities have tended to be overlooked when thinking about diverse approaches to knowledge forms and new directions for social work.

The book began by charting the development of anti-racist social work and underpinning knowledge drawn from sociology and race relations. This section of the book outlined the key debates surrounding assimilation and deficit models of black families which entered professional knowledge in social work and in many ways provided the impetus for anti-racist social work practice.

Although anti-racist social work was both promoted and maligned, this perspective made a major contribution to social work by shifting dominant frameworks towards understanding issues of racism, power and structural inequalities. Even though anti-racist social work offered a powerful critique of social work theory and practice, these perspectives provided opportunities to discuss social welfare concerns emerging from black communities themselves as well as lived experiences in the context of societal racism. As mentioned by Keating (1990) black people were claiming a black presence in social work and a space to influence the debates about policy and practice. The black presence in social work included uncovering the histories of social welfare in black communities. These important contributions opened up life stories, histories, cultural heritage and intellectual agendas emerging from black experiences to counterbalance the virtual absence of this material in social work texts. Under the rubric of black perspectives, the social welfare contributions of black communities and lived experiences came to be recognised in the public realm.

Black perspectives have also invited many critiques and concerns about generalised understandings of black communities and the differences within communities. Nevertheless, there is no doubt that anti-racist social work and black perspectives have changed the landscape of social work. For example, the needs and concerns about black children were acknowledged in the 1989 Children Act and, following the 1990 NHS and Community Care Act, guidelines accompanying the Act addressed the needs of black and ethnic minority communities. Research undertaken by the Race Equality Unit and various other bodies has identified areas of social services and social care where changes need to take place and challenged 'colour-blind' approaches in the provision and delivery of services.

Both anti-racist social work and black perspectives represented a key moment in social work history when the damaging effects of discrimination within both the profession and wider society were brought into view. Social work responded in a number of ways, including developing anti-discriminatory models of practice as core principles of social work education, policy and practice.

As the focus on racism in anti-racist social work seemed to take preference overall, there was a concern that other areas of discrimination were being neglected. In this context, social work moved to adopt anti-discriminatory practice as the main framework for understanding social inequalities in society.

From the high presence of black children in public care to current concerns about the new proposals outlined in the Mental Health Bill currently going through Parliament, these issues are major concerns in black communities and for many professionals. One of the features of 21st-century discrimination is that black communities are often differentially impacted by social policies in various ways. This process appears to pay little attention to forms of institutional racism that have been transmitted through institutions over time. For example, although there are concerns from black parents and educators about black children cited in official school exclusions data, and targets set for the reduction of school exclusions generally, there appears to be no obvious strategy to reduce the exclusion of black children in schools.

The introduction of the 2000 Race Relations (Amendment) Act represents a positive move forward by setting out clear policy initiatives that require social services not only to promote positive relations between communities but also to attend to racial equality across service provision and delivery. The emphasis on promoting equality marks a change in areas of social policy and practice because this strategy can contribute to the development of more appropriate services. By promoting equality, social workers are able to direct these strategies towards social cohesion and better relationships between communities.

Social policy provides the framework in which social work operates and a shift towards promoting equality rather than strategies wholly concerned with stamping out discrimination can be adopted in a more practical way as an important step in challenging discrimination and oppression. Many authors have identified the ways in which social welfare provision can reinforce or lessen existing inequalities. It is, therefore, important that social work as a profession continues to ensure that practice does not amplify the harmful effects of discrimination and inequality.

Over the course of several decades, social work as a profession has been subject to important changes in working practices, largely through legislative frameworks, as well as occupational fragmentation. These changes also include the adoption of anti-discriminatory practice and examples of appropriate service provision. However, the progress that has been made is patchy and the current socio-political climate seems less sympathetic to the goals and priorities of the profession. Even in the wake of these challenges, social justice remains a key element of social work's overall mission and concern.

In the day-to-day working environment, it is all too easy to overlook the potential of social work and the opportunities to foster partnerships and harmonious relationships. In recent years, there has been much discussion in public circles about the 'flatness' of the world in terms of high-speed communication and information highways that bring the social realities of people's lives directly into public and private spaces. This means that significant events in what appear to be far away places affect all of us. There are new opportunities as well as challenges for social work to contribute to a better world.

Another main theme of the book has been the changes in social theory and key debates about postmodern theories and their relevance to social work. The author has shown that there are many perspectives from a range of sources that have the potential for uptake into practice. These sources include a range of theoretical and social action approaches emerging from black perspectives. The influence of postmodern theories has brought about a more sophisticated understanding of discrimination and racism by breaking down generalisations and highlighting the experiences of racism in different contexts and situations. Another important dimension in this discussion is that postmodern theories stress the differences between black communities and individual identities. These perspectives on social life have also drawn attention to the relationship between power and knowledge and the way in which knowledge can be silenced or marginalised in various contexts. In many ways, this approach has opened up intellectual spaces where lived experiences can be voiced and new models of research which explore people's own psychological and social strategies. Overall, social work has had difficulties in integrating this new way of thinking about social life into theory and practice. This is in part due to social work's origins based in a universal understanding of knowledge where methods set out for all families could be applied in practice. Nevertheless, postmodern theories have transformed understanding of social life and models of human behaviour to initiate new areas of study many of which are useful for social work.

Summary points

The first two chapters of the book laid the groundwork for the following chapters, which examined children and families, mental health, disability and ageing.

Children and families

Children and families form an important area of social work that often raises professional and public concern. The high presence of black children in the public care system, and fostering and adoption policies, fuelled criticism that social work failed to address issues of discrimination in services and within the profession. Black–led efforts campaigned for change in social work policies and galvanised black professionals and activists to recruit foster and adoptive carers. These efforts influenced social work policy and practice and legislative reforms.

The 1989 Children Act made specific reference to children from black communities and their needs and established principles that an understanding of a child's background should inform all work with children. The strengths of black families, empowerment and partnership entered social work theory and practice. High profile cases of child abuse in black families have brought into the public arena concerns about the protection of black children and the failure of agencies to work together. There is growing recognition that black children experience a differential position in the broader social and political aspects that inform their lives. In this context, there is a pressing need for the integration of a social model of childhood into social work that encourages opportunities to give voice to lived experiences and engage with children to ascertain a deeper understanding of their ordinary lives to afford both recognition and protection. The 2004 Children Act places children at the centre of policy making along the lines of a multidisciplinary approach to the provision of services. These legislative reforms provide an opportunity for greater appreciation of the wider social contexts which often hinder the well-being of black children.

Mental health

Mental health is another area of controversy in black communities and there is a long-standing concern about the high presence of black people in mental health services. Mental health services have been criticised for many years about the tendency for black people to be detained in hospital and given medication with limited access to alternatives. With the development of service user groups, black service users have voiced their experiences of existing mental health services and what needs to be changed. Despite underfunding, black voluntary organisations are providing services that have adopted a recovery model that includes cultural approaches and insights from black psychology together with a more holistic and spiritual understanding of well-being. There is renewed unease about the proposals in the forthcoming Mental Health Act that allow for compulsory medication to be given in the community. Many black voluntary organisations, including Black Mental Health UK, have called for the integration of the 2000 Race Relations (Amendment) Act to be included in these new proposals so that race equality issues are prioritised.

Disability

The medical model of disability shaped the design of services for people with disabilities until the disability movement challenged this way of understanding social, economic and environmental structures that impede the well-being of people with disabilities. Although social work has adopted the social model of disability there are vestiges of the medical model and individualised approaches which continue to shape service delivery. The social model of disability tends to represent people with disabilities in a general way without references to the differences among people with disabilities. Black people with disabilities experience multiple oppressions and in the past the term 'double jeopardy' has been used to describe their experiences. Black disabled people consider a more sophisticated understanding of the interlocking nature of discrimination can more fully describe their lived experiences.

The introduction of direct payments has clearly encouraged the independence of people with disabilities. However, for black people with disabilities there are complex issues that relate to the notion of independence and personal autonomy because their families and social networks sometimes act as a buffer against the harsh social realities of life.

Although there have been considerable steps forward for people with disabilities generally, there is much work to do in social work practice to meet the needs and aspirations of black disabled people.

Ageing

As more people are living longer into old age, this area of practice has developed through the expansion of services. Social work and social care has drawn upon gerontology to inform models of practice. Black older people are a growing group of older people in British society, and the social inequalities experienced by social groups over the lifespan impact on people in old age. For example, women continue to experience inequalities in the labour market and they are particularly vulnerable to poverty in old age. In a similar way, black older people are likely to experience social and economic disadvantage due to higher rates of unemployment and low levels of income in black communities.

There is evidence that black people experience more ill health with higher rates of physical ill health. The issues of migration and the complexities of ageing in a second homeland and the need to fully understand the implications of migration for social work formed an important theme in Chapter Seven. Models of ageing have been popular in attempting to understand the process of ageing. However, these models tend to present a general understanding that often overlooks many issues concerning black older people. Models of ageing have been slow to include issues of migration, culture and the specific circumstances of black older people, and, in particular, the cultural implications of growing old and how to translate these factors into appropriate services. Life history work and oral history continue to play an important part in preserving first-hand accounts of histories of black communities in Britain and this method can be an empowering experience for black older people.

The introduction of new standards for the care of older people are welcomed but more attention should be placed on the needs of black older people and more access to relevant information to ensure better outcomes.

In closing, the author hopes that this book will contribute to the many exciting developments as social work begins to embrace culturally diverse models of practice.

References

ABSWAP (Association of Black Social Workers and Allied Professions) (1983) *Black children in care*, Evidence to the House of Commons Social Services Committee.

Acker, J. (1992) 'Gendering organisational theory', in A. Mills and P. Tancred (eds) *Gendering organisational analysis*, Thousand Oaks, CA: Sage Publications.

Adams, R. (2002) *Social policy for social work*, Basingstoke: Palgrave.

Adams, R. (2003) *Social work and empowerment* (3rd edn), Basingstoke: Palgrave.

Adams, R., Dominelli, L. and Payne, M. (2002a) *Social work: Themes, Issues and Critical Debates, 2nd edn*, Basingstoke: Palgrave.

Adams, R., Dominelli, L. and Payne, M. (2002b) *Critical Practice in Social Work*, Basingstoke: Palgrave.

Ahmad, B. (1989) 'Childcare and ethnic minorities', in B. Khan (ed) *Child care research, policy and practice*, London: Hodder & Stoughton and Open University.

Ahmad, B. (1990) *Black perspectives in social work*, Birmingham: Venture Press.

Ahmad, W.I.U. (1996) 'Family obligations and social change among Asian communities', in K. Atkins (ed) *'Race' and community care*, Buckingham: Open University Press.

Ahmad W.I.U. (ed) (2000) *Ethnicity, disability and chronic illness*, Buckingham: Open University Press.

Ahmad, W.I.U. and Atkins, K. (1996) *Race and community care*, Buckingham: Open University Press.

Ahmed, S. (2005) 'What is the evidence of early intervention? Preventative services for black and minority ethnic group children and their families', *Practice*, vol 17, no 2, pp 89-102.

Alcock, P. (1993) *Understanding poverty* (2nd edn), Basingstoke: Palgrave.

Alvesson, M. (2002) *Postmodernism and social research*, Buckingham: Open University Press.

Andersen, M. and Hill-Collins, P. (2004) *Race, class and gender: An anthology* (5th edn), Belmont, CA: Wadsworth/Thomson Learning.

Andersson, L. and Oberg, P. (2004) 'Diversity, health and ageing', in S.O. Daatland and S. Biggs (eds) *Ageing and diversity*, Bristol: The Policy Press.

Anthony, W.A. (1993) 'Recovery from mental illness: the guiding vision of the mental health system in the 1990s', *Psychological Rehabilitation Journal*, vol 16, pp 11-24.

Audit Commission (2003) *Journey to race equality*, London: Audit Commission.

Bagihole, B. (1997) *Equal opportunities and social policy: Issues of gender, 'race' and disability*, London: Longman.

Baldock, J. (1993) 'Old age', in R. Dallos and E. McLaughlin (eds) *Social problems and the family*, London: Open University Press/Sage Publications.

Banks, N. (1999a) *White counsellors – Black clients: Theory, research and practice*, Aldershot: Ashgate.

Banks, N. (1999b) 'Direct identity work', in R. Barn (ed) *Working with black children and adolescents in need*, London: British Association for Fostering and Adoption.

Banks, S. (2001) *Ethics and values in social work* (2nd edn), Basingstoke: Palgrave.

Banton, M. (1972) *Racial minorities*, London: Fontana.

Barn, R. (1993) *Black children in the public care system*, London: Batsford.

Barn, R. (2001) 'Black families and children: planning to meet their needs', *Research and Policy Planning*, vol 17, no 2, pp 5-11.

Barn, R., Andrew, L. and Mantovani, N. (2005) *Life after care: The experiences of young people from different ethnic groups*, London: Joseph Rowntree Foundation.

Barn, R., Sinclair, R. and Ferdinand, D. (1997) *Acting on principle: An examination of race and ethnicity in social services provision for children and families*, London: British Association for Adoption and Fostering.

Barnes, M. and Bowl, R. (2001) *Taking over the asylum: Empowerment and mental health*, Basingstoke: Palgrave Macmillan.

Bebbington, A.C. and Miles, J.B. (1989) 'The background of children who enter local authority care', *British Journal of Social Work*, vol 19, no 5, pp 349-68.

Beck, U. (1998) 'Politics of risk society', in J. Franklin (ed) *The politics of risk society*, Cambridge: Polity.

Belgrave, F. and Allison, K. (2005) *African American psychology*, Thousand Oaks, CA: Sage Publications.

Beresford, P. and Croft, S. (2001) 'Service users' knowledges and the social construction of social work', *Journal of Social Work*, vol 1, no 3, pp 295-316.

Bernard, C. (2001) *Constructing lived experiences: Representations of black mothers in child sexual abuse discourses*, Aldershot: Ashgate Publishing.

Bernard, C. (2002) 'Giving voice to experiences: parental mistreatment of black children in the context of societal racism', *Journal of Child and Family Social Work*, vol 7, no 4, pp 239-53.

Berthoud, R. (2002) 'Poverty and prosperity among Britain's ethnic minorities', *Benefits*, vol 10, no 1, pp 3-8.

Bhavnani, R., Mirza, H.S. and Meetoo, V. (2005) *Tackling the roots of racism*, Bristol: The Policy Press.

Bhuik, K. (2002) *Racism and mental health*, London: Jessica Kingsley.

Biehal, N., Wade, J., Clayden, J. and Stein, M. (1995) *Moving on: Young people and leaving care schemes*, London: HMSO.

Biggs, S. (2004) 'New ageism: age imperialism, personal experience and ageing policy', in S.O. Daatland and S. Biggs (eds) *Ageing and diversity*, Bristol: The Policy Press.

Billingsley, A. (1968) *Black families in white America*, Englewood, NJ: Prentice Hall.

Black and In Care (1984) *Black and in care: Conference report*, Blackrose Press.

Blakemore, K. and Boneham, M. (1994) *Age, Race and Ethnicity: A comparative approach*, Buckingham: Open University Press.

Blom-Cooper, L. (1985) *A Child in Trust: A Report of the Panel of Inquiry into Circumstances Surrounding the Death of Jasmine Beckford*, London: London Borough of Brent.

Bornat, J. (1998) 'Approaches to reminiscence', in M. Allott and M. Robb (eds) *Understanding health and social care*, London: Open University Press/Sage Publications.

Bowling, B. and Phillips, C. (2002) *Racism, crime and justice*, Harlow: Pearson Education Ltd.

Brah, A. (2000) 'Difference, diversity and differentiation', in K. Bhavnani (ed) *Feminism and race*, Oxford: Oxford University Press.

Brake, M. and Bailey, R. (1980) *Radical social work*, London: Edward Arnold.

Braye, S. and Preston-Shoot, M. (1995) *Empowering practice in social care*, Buckingham: Open University Press.

BASW (British Association of Social Workers) (25 April 2003) *Code of ethics* (http://basw.co.uk/articles.php?articleId=2).

Broad, B. (2005) 'Young people leaving care: implementing the Children (Leaving Care) Act 2000?', *Children and Society*, vol 19, no 5, pp 371-84.

Brophy, J. (2003) 'Diversity and child protection', *Family Law Review*, September, pp 674-9.

Brown, C. (1992) '"Same difference": the persistence of racial disadvantage in the British employment market', in P. Braham, A. Rattansi and R. Skellington (eds) *Racism and antiracism, inequalities, opportunities, and policies*, London: Open University/Sage Publications.

Brown, K. (ed) (2005) *Encyclopedia of language and linguistics*, 2nd edition, vols 1-14, St Louis, MO: Elsevier Science.

Bryan, B., Dadzie, S. and Scafe, S. (1985) *The heart of the race: Black women's lives in Britain*, London: Virgo.

Bullis, R. (1996) *Spirituality in social work practice*, Washington, DC: Taylor Francis.

Butt, J. (1994) *Same service or equal service?*, London: HMSO.

Butt, J. and O'Neil, A. (2004) *Let's move on: Black and minority ethnic older people's views on research findings*, London: Joseph Rowntree Foundation.

Butt, J., Patel, B. and Stuart, O. (2005) *Race equality discussion papers*, London: Social Care Institute for Excellence.

Cabinet Office (2000) *Winning the generation game*, London: Cabinet Office.

Cameron, E., Badger, F. and Evers, H. (1996) 'Ethnicity and care management', in J. Phillips and B. Penhale (eds) *Reviewing care management for older people*, London: Jessica Kingsley.

Carby, H. (1982) 'White women listen! Black feminism and the boundaries of sisterhood', in Centre for Contemporary Cultural Studies, *The empire strikes back*, London: Hutchinson.

CCCS (Centre for Contemporary Cultural Studies) (1982) *The empire strikes back*, London: Hutchinson.

Carter, J., Fenton, S. and Modood, T. (1999) *Ethnicity and employment in higher education*, London: Policy Studies Institute.

CCETSW (Central Council for Education and Training in Social Work) (1989) *Requirements and regulations for the Diploma in Social Work*, Paper 30, London: CCETSW.

CCETSW (1991) *Requirements and regulations for the Diploma in Social Work* (2nd edn), Paper 30, London: CCETSW.

CCETSW (1995) *Requirements and regulations for the Diploma in Social Work* (revised), London: CCETSW.

Chand, A. (2000) 'The over-representation of Black children in the child protection system: possible causes, consequences and solutions" *Child and Family Social Work*, vol 5, no 1, pp 67-77.

Chand, A. (2005) 'Do you speak English? Language barriers in child protection with minority ethnic families', *British Journal of Social Work*, vol 35, no 6, pp 807-21.

Channer, Y. and Parton, N. (1990) 'Racism, cultural relativism and child protection', in Violence against Children Study Group, *Taking child abuse seriously*, London: Unwin Hyman.

Cheetham, J. (1982) *Social work services for ethnic minorities in Britain and the USA*, London: DHSS.

Chouhan, K. and Lusane, C. (2004) *Black voluntary and community sector funding: Its impact on civic engagement and capacity building*, York: Joseph Rowntree Foundation.

Christensen, P. and Prout, A. (2005) 'Anthropological and sociological perspectives on the study of children', in S. Greene and D. Hogan (eds) *Researching children's experience*, Thousand Oaks, CA: Sage Publications.

Christian, M. (2004) 'Philosophy and practice for Black studies', in M. Kete Asante and M. Karenga (eds) *Handbook of Black studies*, Thousand Oaks, CA: Sage Publications.

Clark, J. (2003) *Independence matters*, London: DH.

Coleman, P.G. (1974) 'Measuring reminiscence characteristics from conversation as adaptive features of old age', *International Journal of Aging and Human Development*, vol 5, pp 281-94.

Cox, C.B. and Ephross, P.H. (1998) *Ethnicity and social work practice*, New York, NY: Oxford University Press.

Croft, S. and Beresford, P. (2002) 'Service users' perspectives', in M. Davies (ed) *The Blackwell companion to social work*, (2nd edn), Oxford: Blackwell Publishers.

Cross, W.E. (1978) 'The Thomas and Cross models of psychological nigrescence: a literature review', *The Journal of Black Psychology*, vol 5, no 1, pp 13-27.

Cross, W.E. (1980) 'Models of psychological nigrescence: a literature review', in R.L. Jones (ed) *Black psychology* (2nd edn), Los Angeles, CA: Cobb and Henry.

Crozier, G. (2001) 'Excluded parents: the deracialization of parental involvement', *Race, Ethnicity and Education*, vol 4, no 4, pp 329-41.

Dalrymple, J. and Burke, B. (1995) *Anti-oppressive practice: Social care and the law*, Buckingham: Open University Press.

Daniel, B., Featherstone, B., Hooper, C.-A. and Scourfield, J. (2005) 'Why gender matters for *Every Child Matters*', *British Journal of Social Work*, vol 35, no 8, pp 1343-55.

Dei, G. (1999) 'Rethinking the role of indigenous knowledges in the academy', Public Lecture, Department of Sociology and Equity Studies, University of Toronto, Canada.

Dei, G. (2005) 'Antiracism: theorizing in the context of perils and desires', in M.K. Asante and M. Karenga (eds) *Handbook of Black studies*, Thousand Oak, CA: Sage Publications, pp 107-15.

Devore, W. and Schlesinger, E.G. (1999) *Ethnic-sensitive social work practice*, Boston, MA: Allyn and Bacon.

DH (Department of Health) (1990) *Community care in the next decade and beyond: Policy guidance*, London: HMSO.

DH (1995a) *The challenge of partnership in child protection*, London: HMSO.

DH (1995b) *Child protection and Child abuse: Messages from Research*, London: HMSO.

DH (1999) *National Service Framework for mental health: Modern standards and service models*, London: DH.

DH (2000) *A quality strategy for social care*, London: DH.

DH (2001a) *The journey to recovery: The government's vision for mental healthcare*, London: DH.

DH (2001b) *National Service Framework for older people*, London: DH.

DH (2003) *Inside, outside: Improving mental health services for black and minority ethnic communities*, London: DH.

DfES (2004) *Every Child Matters: The Next Steps*, London: The Stationery Office.

Dominelli, L. (1988) *Anti-racist social work*, Basingstoke: Palgrave Macmillan.

Dominelli, L. (2002) *Anti-oppressive social work theory and practice*, Basingstoke: Palgrave.

DuBois, B. and K.K. Miley (2002) *Social work: An empowering profession*, Boston MA: Allyn and Bacon.

DuBois, W.E.B. (1903) *The souls of black folks*, New York, NY: Penguin Books.

Enriquez, J. (2005) *The untied states of America, polarization, fracturing, and our future*, New York, NY: Crown Publishers.

Essed, P. (1991) *Understanding everyday racism: An interdisciplinary theory*, Newbury Park, CA: Sage Publications.

Estes, C. (2001) *Social policy and aging*, Thousand Oaks, CA: Sage Publications.

Estes, C., Biggs, S. and Phillipson, C. (2003) *Social theory, social policy and ageing*, Buckingham: Open University Press.

Evans, R. and Banton, M. (2000) *Learning from experience: Involving black disabled people in shaping services*, Leamington Spa: Counsel of Disabled People.

Fanon, F. (1967) *Black skin, white masks*, London: Pluto Press.

Fernando, S. (2001) *Mental health, race and culture*, Basingstoke: Palgrave Macmillan.

Fine, M., Weis, L., Powell, L. and Mun Wong, L. (eds) (1997) *Off white: Readings on race, power and society*, New York, NY: Routledge.

First Key (1987) *A study of young black people leaving care*, London: Commission for Racial Equality.

Fluehr-Lobban, C. (2006) *Race and racism: An introduction*, Lanham, MD: Rowman and Littlefield.

Fook, J. (2002) *Social work critical theory and practice*, London: Sage Publications.

Forbat, L. (2004) 'The care and abuse of minoritised ethnic groups: the role of statutory services', *Critical Social Policy*, vol 24, no 3, pp 312-31.

Frankenberg, R. (1997) 'Introduction: local whiteness, localizing whiteness', in R. Frankenberg (ed) *Displacing whiteness: Essays in social and cultural criticism*, Durham, NC: Duke University Press.

Frederick, J. (1995) *Reachin' out: Developing a community mental health service for African Caribbean people*, London: ISIS, The Black Mental Health Group.

Fredman, S. (2001) 'Combating racism with human rights: the right to equality', in S. Fredman (ed) *Discrimination and human rights: The case of racism*, Oxford: Oxford University Press.

Friedman, T. (2005) *The world is flat, a brief history of the 21st century*, New York, NY: Farrar, Straus and Giroux.

Fryer, P. (1984) *Staying power: The history of black people in Britain*, London: Pluto Press.

Furness, S. (2005) 'Shifting sands: developing cultural competence', *Practice*, vol 17, no 4, pp 247-56.

Garrett, P. (2004) 'More trouble with Harry: a rejoinder in the "life politics" debate', *British Journal of Social Work*, vol 34, no 4, pp 577-89.

Gil, D. (1994) 'Confronting social injustice and oppression', in F. Reamer (ed) *The foundations of social work knowledge*, New York, NY: Columbia University Press.

Gil, D. (1998) *Confronting injustice and oppression: Concepts and strategies for social workers*, New York, NY: Columbia University Press.

Gillborn, D. (2001) 'Racism, policy and the (mis)education of black children', in R. Majors (ed) *Educating our black children*, London: Routledge/Falmer.

Gillborn, D. (2004) 'Racism, policy and contemporary schooling: current inequities and future possibilities', *Sage Race Relations Abstracts*, vol 29, no 2, pp 5-33.

Goddard, J. (2003) 'Children leaving care in the United Kingdom: "corporate parenting" and social exclusion', *Journal of Societal and Social Policy*, vol 2/3, pp 21-34.

Goffman, E. (1961) *Asylums: Essays on the social situation of mental health patients and other inmates*, Harmondsworth: Penguin.

Goldstein, B. (1999) 'Black, with a white parent, a positive and achievable identity', *British Journal of Social Work*, vol 29, no 2, pp 285-301.

Goldstein, B. (2002) 'Black perspectives', in M. Davies (ed) *The Blackwell companion to social work*, Oxford: Blackwell Publishers.

Golightley, M. (2004) *Social work and mental health*, Exeter: Learning Matters Ltd.

Gordon, G. (2001) 'Transforming lives: towards bicultural competence', in P. Reason and H. Bradbury (eds) *Handbook of action research*, Thousand Oaks, CA: Sage Publications, pp 314-23.

Gordon, P. (1995) 'The fringe dwellers: African American women scholars in the postmodern era', in B. Kanpol and P. McLaren (eds) *Critical multiculturalism: Uncommon voices in a common struggle*, Westport, CT: Bergin and Garvey.

Graham, M. (1999) 'The African-centred worldview: developing a paradigm for social work', *British Journal of Social Work*, vol 29, no 2, pp 252-67.

Graham, M. (2002) *Social work and African-centred worldviews*, Birmingham: BASW/Venture Press.

Graham, M. (2004) 'Empowerment revisited – social work, resistance and agency in Black communities', *European Journal of Social Work*, vol 7, no 1, pp 43-56.

Graham, M. (2005) 'Maat: an African centered paradigm for psychological and spiritual healing', in R. Moodley and W. West (eds) *Integrating traditional and cultural healing practices in counseling and psychotherapy*, Thousand Oaks, CA: Sage Publications.

Graham, M. (2006a) 'Giving voice to black children: an analysis of social agency', *British Journal of Social Work*, first published on 22 August, doi:10.1093/bjsw/bc1084.

Graham, M. (2006b) 'Black studies and the social work paradigm: implications of a new analysis', in M. Asante and M. Karenga (eds) *Handbook of Black Studies*, Thousand Oaks, CA: Sage Publications, pp 304-16.

Graham, M. (2007) 'Knowledge representation in social work education', *The International Journal of the Humanities*, vol 3, no 10, pp 9-14.

Graham, M. and Bruce, E. (2006) '"Seen and not heard" – sociological approaches to childhood: black children, agency and implications for child welfare', *Journal of Sociology and Social Welfare*, vol 34, no 4, pp 31-48.

Graham, M. and Robinson, G. (2004) '"The silent catastrophe" – Institutional racism and the underachievement of Black boys in the British educational system', *Journal of Black Studies*, vol 37, no 5, pp 653-71.

Groce, N. (1988) *Everyone here spoke sign language*, Cambridge, MA: Harvard University Press.

Groce, N. (2005) 'Immigrants, disability and rehabilitation', in J. Stone (ed) *Culture and disability*, Thousand Oaks, CA: Sage Publications.

Gutierrez, L.M., Parsons, R.J. and Cox, E.O. (1998) *Empowerment in social work practice: A sourcebook*, Pacific Grove, CA: Brooks/Cole.

Hall, S. (1992) 'New ethnicities', in J. Donald and A. Rattansi (eds) *Race, culture and difference*, London: Sage Publications.

Harris, V. (1991) 'Values of social work in the context of the British society in conflict with anti-racism', in CD Project Steering Group (eds) *Setting the context for change*, London: CCETSW.

Hasler, F. (2004) 'Direct payments', in J. Swain, S. French, S. Barnes and C. Thomas (eds) *Disabling barriers – Enabling environments* (2nd edn), London: Sage Publications.

HEA (Health Education Authority) (1997) *Mental health promotion: A quality framework*, London: HEA.

Healy, K. (2000) *Social work practices*, Thousand Oaks, CA: Sage Publications.

Healy, K. (2001) 'Reinventing critical social work: challenges from practice, context and postmodernism', *Critical Social Work*, vol 2, no 1, pp 1-13.

Heffernan, K. (2006) 'Social work, new public management and the language of "service user"', *British Journal of Social Work*, vol 36, no 1, pp 139-47.

Hick, S., Fook, J. and Puzzuto, R. (eds) (2005) *Social work: A critical turn*, Toronto: Thompson Educational Publishing Inc.

Hill, R.B. (1971) *The strengths of black families*, New York, NY: Emerson Hall.

Hill-Collins, P. (1989) 'The social construction of black feminist thought', *Signs, Journal of Women in Culture and Society*, vol 14, no 4, pp 745-773.

Hill-Collins, P. (1991) *Black feminist thought: Knowledge, consciousness and the politics of empowerment*, London: Routledge.

hooks, b. (1984) *Feminist theory: From margin to centre*, Boston, MA: South End Press.

Hopton, J. (1997) 'Anti-discriminatory practice and anti-oppressive practice', *Critical Social Policy*, no 52, vol 17, pp 47-61.

Howitt, D. and Owusu-Bempah, J. (1990) *The racism of psychology: Time for change*, Hemel Hempstead: Harvester Wheatsheaf.

Humphreys, C., Atkar, S. and Baldwin, S. (1999) 'Discrimination in child protection work: recurring themes in work with Asian families', *Child and Family Social Work*, vol 4, no 4, pp 283-91.

Ince, L. (1998) *Making it alone: A study of the care experiences of young people*, London: British Association for Adoption and Fostering

Ince, L. (1999) 'Preparing young black people for leaving care', in R. Barn (ed) *Working with black children and adolescents in need*, London: British Association for Adoption and Fostering.

Ince, L. (2004) 'Young black people leaving care', in V. Lewis, M. Kellett, C. Robinson, S. Fraser and S. Ding (eds) *The reality of research with children and young people*, London: Sage Publications.

Jacobs, B. (1986) *Black politics and urban crisis*, Cambridge: Cambridge University Press.

Johnson, P. (2006) 'Blair: Paying religious groups is a mistake', *The Daily Telegraph*, 9 December (www.telegraph.co.uk/news/main.jhtml?xml=/news/2006/12/08/ublair108.xm).

Keating, F. and Robertson, D. (2004) 'Fear, black people and mental illness: a vicious circle?', *Health and Social Care in the Community*, vol 12, no 5, pp 439-47.

Kim, J. (1981) 'Process of Asian-American identity development: a study of Japanese American women's perception of their struggle to achieve positive identities', unpublished doctoral dissertation, Amherst, University of Massachusetts.

King, A. (1994) 'An Afrocentric cultural awareness program for incarcerated African-American males', *Journal of Multicultural Social Work*, vol 3, no 4, pp 17-28.

Kirton, G. and Greene, A. (2000) *The dynamics of managing diversity – A critical approach*, Oxford: Butterworth Heinemann.

Krieken, R. (1999) 'The "stolen generations" and cultural genocide', *Childhood*, vol 6, no 3, pp 297-311.

Laming, H. (2003) *The Victoria Climbié Inquiry: Report by Lord Laming*, Cm 5730, London: The Stationery Office.

Lawrence, E. (1982) 'Just plain common sense: the "roots" of racism', in Centre for Contemporary Cultural Studies, *The empire strikes back*, London: Hutchinson.

Lee, C., Oh, M. and Mountcastle, A. (1992) 'Indigenous models of helping in non-western countries: implications for multicultural counseling', *Journal of Multicultural Counseling and Development*, vol 20, pp 1-10.

Lester, H. and Glasby, J. (2006) *Mental health policy and practice*, Basingstoke: Palgrave Macmillan.

London Borough of Lambeth (1987) *Whose child? The Report of the Public Inquiry into the Death of Tyra Henry*, London: London Borough of Lambeth.

Long, A., Grayson, L. and Boaz, A. (2006) 'Assessing the quality of knowledge in social care: exploring the potential of a set of generic standards', *British Journal of Social Work*, vol 36, no 2, pp 207-26.

Longmore, P. (1993) 'History of the disability rights movement and disability culture', unpublished address to the California Disability Leadership Summit, October 11, Anaheim, CA.

Lorimer, D. (1992) 'Black resistance to slavery and racism in eighteenth century England', in J. Gundasra and I. Duffield (eds) *Essays on the history of blacks in Britain*, Aldershot: Ashgate.

Lymberry, M. and Butler, S. (2004) *Social work: Ideals and practice*, Basingstoke: Palgrave Macmillan.

McDonald, A. (2006) *Understanding community care: A guide for social workers*, Basingstoke: Palgrave Macmillan.

McIntosh, P. (2004) 'White privilege: Unpacking the invisible knapsack', in M. Anderson and P. Hill-Collins (eds) *Race, class and gender: An anthology*, Belmont, CA: Wadsworth Publishing Co.

McLeod, M., Owen, D. and Khamis, C. (2001) *Black and minority ethnic voluntary and community organisations: Their role and future development in England and Wales*, London: Policy Studies Institute.

Macpherson, W. (1999) *Stephen Lawrence Inquiry: Report of an Inquiry by Sir William Macpherson of Cluny*, Cm 4262-I, London: The Stationery Office.

McVeigh T. and Hill, A. (2005) 'Racists axe black teenager to death', *The Observer*, 31 July.

Macey, M. and Moxon, E. (1996) 'An examination of anti-racist and anti-oppressive theory and practice in social work education', *British Journal of Social Work*, vol 26, no 2, pp 297-314.

Manning, M., Cornelius, L. and Okundaye, J. (2004) 'Empowering African Americans through social work practice: integrating an Afrocentric perspective, ego psychology, and spirituality', *Families in Society*, vol 34, no 4, pp 229-35.

Maxime, J. (1987) 'Racial identity – its value to black children', *Social Work Today*, 15 June.

Maxime, J. (1993) 'The importance of racial identity for the psychological well being of Black children', *ACPP Review and Newsletter*, vol 15, no 4, pp 173-9.

Mental Health Act Commission (1997) *7th biennial report: 1995-1997*, London: The Stationery Office.

Mizra, H. (1997) *Black British feminism: A reader*, London: Routledge.

Modood, T., Berthoud, R. and Nazroo, J. (1997) *Diversity and disadvantage, Fourth National Survey of Ethnic Minorities*, London: Policy Studies Institute.

Moodley, R. and West, W. (eds) (2005) *Integrating traditional healing practices into counseling and psychotherapy*, Thousand Oaks, CA: Sage Publications.

Moody, H.R. (2001) 'Productive ageing and the ideology of old age', in N. Morrow-Howell, J. Hinterlong and M. Sherranden (eds) *Productive ageing: Concepts and challenges*, Thousand Oaks, CA: Pine Forge Press, pp 175-96.

Mullaly, B. (2001) 'Confronting the politics of despair: toward the reconstruction of progressive social work in a global economy and postmodern age', *Social Work Education*, vol 20, no 3, pp 303-20.

Mydral, G. (1944) *An American dilemma: The Negro problem and modern democracy*, New York, NY: Harper.

Myers, L. (1988) *Understanding an Afrocentric world-view: Introduction to an optimal psychology*, Dubuque, IA: Kendall/Hunt.

Myers, N. (1993) 'Servant, sailor, tailor, beggarman: black survival in white society 1780-1830', *Immigrants and Minorities*, vol 12, no 1, pp 47-74.

NCB (National Children's Bureau) (2004) *The care experience: Through black eyes*, London: NCB.

Nobles, W. (1978) 'Toward an empirical and theoretical framework for defining black families', *Journal of Marriage and Family*, vol 40, no 4 pp 679-88.

Nobles, W. (2004) 'African philosophy: foundations for black psychology', in R. Jones (ed) *Black psychology*, Berkeley, CA: Cobbs and Henry.

Noble, D. (2005) 'Remembering bodies, healing histories: the emotional politics of everyday freedom', in C. Alexander and C. Knowles (eds) *Making race matter: Bodies, space and identity*, Basingstoke: Palgrave Macmillan.

ODPM (Office of the Deputy Prime Minister) (2003) *Equality and diversity in local government*, July, London: ODPM (www.local.odpm. gov.uk/research/crosscut/crosscut.htm).

O'Hagan, K. (1999) 'Culture, cultural identity, and cultural sensitivity in child and family social work', *Child and Family Social Work*, vol 4, no 4, pp 269-81.

O'Hagan, K. (2001) *Cultural competence in the caring professions*, London: Jessica Kingsley Publishers.

Oliver, M. (1990) *The politics of disablement*, London: Macmillan.

Oliver, M. (1993) 'Disability and dependency: a creation of industrial societies?', in J. Swain, V. Finkelstein, S. French and M. Oliver (eds) *Disabling barriers – Enabling environments*, London: Sage Publications.

Oliver, M. (1996) *Understanding disability*, London: Macmillan.

Oliver, M. and Sapey, B. (2006) *Social work with disabled people* (3rd edn), Basingstoke: Palgrave Macmillan.

ONS (Office for National Statistics) (2003) *Census 2001: National Report for England and Wales*, London: The Stationery Office.

Owusu-Bempah, J. (1997) 'Race', in M. Davies (ed) *The Blackwell companion to social work*, Oxford: Blackwell Publishers.

Parham, T. (ed) (2002) *Counseling persons of African descent*, Thousand Oaks, CA: Sage Publications.

Parton, N. (1985) *The politics of child abuse*, Basingstoke: Macmillan.

Pawson, R., Boaz, A., Grayson, L., Long, A.F. and Barnes, C. (2003) *Types and quality of knowledge in social care*, London: Social Care Institute for Excellence.

Payne, M. (2005) *Modern social work theory*, Basingstoke: Palgrave Macmillan.

Penketh, L. (2000) *Tackling institutional racism*, Bristol: The Policy Press.

Perkins, R. (2003) 'Economic and social inclusion', *Openmind magazine*, May/June, issue 121, p 6.

Phillips, J., Ray, M. and Marshall, M. (2006) *Social work with older people* (4th edn), Basingstoke: Palgrave Macmillan.

Phillipson, C. and Ahmed, N. (2004) 'Transnational communities, migration and changing identities in later life: a new research agenda', in S.O. Daatland and S. Biggs (eds) *Ageing and diversity*, Bristol: The Policy Press.

Phoenix, A. (1997) '"I'm white! So what?" The construction of whiteness for young Londoners', in M. Fine, L. Weiss, L. Powell and L. Mun Wong (eds) *Off white: Readings on race, power and society*, London: Routledge.

Pilkington, A. (2003) *Racial disadvantage and ethnic diversity in Britain*, Basingstoke: Palgrave.

Rai-Atkins, A. (2002) *Best practice in mental health: Advocacy for African, Caribbean and South Asian communities*, Bristol/York: The Policy Press/ Joseph Rowntree Foundation.

Raleigh, V.S. (2000) 'Mental health in black and ethnic minorities', in C. Kaye and T. Lingialy (eds) *Race, culture and ethnicity in secure psychiatric practice*, London: Jessica Kingsley.

Ray, M. and Phillips, J. (2002) 'Older people', in R. Adams, L. Dominelli and M. Payne (eds) *Critical practice in social work*, Basingstoke: Palgrave Macmillan.

Reamer, F. (1993) *The philosophical foundations of social work*, New York, NY: Columbia University Press.

Reamer, F. (1998) 'The evolution of social work ethics', *Social Work*, vol 43, no 6, pp 488-98.

Reid-Galloway, C. (2002) *Fact Sheet: The African Caribbean community and mental health in Britain*, London: Mind.

Richards, M. (2006) 'Uncertain age', *The Guardian*, 23 August.

Rigg, C. and Trehan, K. (1999) 'Not critical enough? Black women raise challenges for critical management learning', *Gender and Education*, vol 11, no 3, pp 265-80.

Robinson, G. (2006) 'Equal opportunities and managing diversity', in W. Bolosi (ed) *Human Resource Management*, London: McGraw-Hill.

Robinson, L. (1995) *Psychology for social workers: Black perspectives*, London: Routledge.

Robinson, L. (2000) 'Racial identity, attitudes and self-esteem of black adolescents in residential care: an exploratory study', *British Journal of Social Work*, vol 30, no 1, pp 3-24.

Rose, E.J.B. (1969) *Colour and citizenship: A report on British race relations*, London: Oxford University Press.

Rowe, J. and Lambert, L. (1973) *Children who wait*, London: British Association for Adoption and Fostering.

Rowe, J., Hundleby, M. and Garnett, L. (1989) *Child care now*, London: British Association for Adoption and Fostering.

Rustin, M. (2005) 'Conceptual analysis of critical moments in Victoria Climbié's life', *Child and Family Social Work*, vol 10, no 1, pp 11-19.

Salsgiver, R. (2006) Power point presentation, California State University, Fresno, California.

Sandbaek, M. (1999) 'Children with problems: focusing on everyday life', *Children and Society*, vol 13, no 2, pp 106-18.

Sarup, M. (1988) *An introductory guide to post-structuralism and post-modernism*, Hemel Hempstead: Harvester Wheatsheaf.

Sayce, L. (1995) *Response to violence – A framework for fair treatment in psychiatric patient risk and response*, London: Gerald Duckworth and Co Ltd.

Schiele, J. (2000) *Human services and the Afrocentric paradigm*, New York, NY: Haworth Press.

SEU (Social Exclusion Unit) (1998) *Rough sleeping*, London: The Stationery Office.

Sheppard, M. (2002) 'Mental health and social justice: gender, race and psychological consequences of unfairness', *British Journal of Social Work*, vol 32, no 6, pp 779-97.

Singh, G. (1992) *Race and social work from 'black pathology' to 'black perspectives'*, Bradford: Race Relations Research Unit.

Sivanandan, A. (1983) 'Challenging racism: strategies for the eighties', *Race and Class*, no 25, pp 1-2.

Skellington, R. and Morris, P. (1992) *'Race' in Britain today*, London: Sage Publications.

Small, J. (1982) 'New black families', *Adoption and Fostering*, BAAF, vol 6, pp 3-35.

Small, J. (1984) 'The crisis in adoption', *International Journal of Social Psychiatry*, vol 30, no 1/2, Spring, pp 129-142.

Solomon, B. (1976) *Black empowerment: Social work in oppressed communities*, New York, NY: Columbia University Press.

Solomos, J. and Bulmer, M. (2004) *Researching race and racism*, London: Routledge.

Stein, M. (1997) *What works in leaving care?*, London: Barnardo's.

Stepney, P. (2006) 'Mission impossible? Critical practice in social work', *British Journal of Social Work*, vol 36, no 8, pp 1289-307.

Stuart, O. (1993) 'Double oppression: an appropriate starting point?', in J. Swain, V. Finkelstein, S. French and M. Oliver (eds) *Disabling barriers – Enabling environments*, London: Sage Publications/Open University.

Stuart, O. (1996) '"Yes, we mean black disabled people too": thoughts on community care and disabled people from black and minority ethnic communities', in W.I.U. Ahmad and K. Atkins (eds) *Race and community care*, Buckingham: Open University Press.

Stuart, O. (2005) 'How can independent living become a viable option for black and minority ethnic service users and carers?', in J. Butt, B. Patel and O. Stuart (eds) *Race equality discussion papers*, London: Social Care Institute for Excellence.

Stuart, O. (2006) 'Fear and loathing in front of a mirror', in C. Alexander and C. Knowles (eds) *Making race matters: Bodies, space and identity*, Basingstoke: Palgrave Macmillan.

Sue, D.W. (2006) *Multicultural social work practice*, Hoboken, NJ: John Wiley and Sons Inc.

Swain, J., French, S. and Cameron, C. (2005) *Controversial issues in a disabling society*, Buckingham: Open University Press.

Swain, J., French, S., Barnes, C. and Thomas, C. (2004) *Disabling barriers – Enabling environments* (2nd edn), London: Sage Publications/Open University.

Taylor, C. (1994) 'The politics of recognition', in A. Gutmann (ed) *Multiculturalism: Examining the politics of recognition*, Princeton, NJ: Princeton University Press.

Taylor, C. (2004) 'Underpinning knowledge for child care practice: reconsidering child development theory', *Child and Family Social Work*, vol 9, no 3, pp 225-35.

Thernstrom, A. and Thernstrom, S. (1999) *America in black and white: One nation indivisible*, Clearwater: FL: Touchstone books.

Thomas, N. (2000) *Children, family and the state*, Basingstoke, Macmillan Press.

Thomas, N. (2005) *Social work with young people in care*, Basingstoke: Palgrave Macmillan.

Thomas, N. and O'Kane, C. (2000) 'Discovering what children think: connections between research and practice', *British Journal of Social Work*, vol 30, no 6, pp 810-35.

Thompson, N. (1993) *Anti-discriminatory practice*, Basingstoke: Macmillan.

Thompson, N. (1997) *Anti-discriminatory practice* (2nd edn), Basingstoke: Macmillan.

Thompson, N. (2003) *Promoting equality*, Basingstoke: Palgrave Macmillan.

Tomlinson, S. (1977) 'Race and education in Britain 1960-1977: an overview of the literature', *Sage Race Relations Abstracts*, vol 2, no 4, pp 3-33.

Torres, S. (2004) 'Making sense of the construct of successful ageing: the migrant experience', in S.O. Daatland and S. Biggs (eds) *Ageing and diversity*, Bristol: The Policy Press.

Trevithick, P. (2005) *Social work skills: A practice handbook* (2nd edn), Buckingham: Open University Press.

T'Shaka, O. (1995) *Return to the African mother principle of male and female equality*, Oakland, CA: Pan Afrikan.

Turner, D. (2006) 'The interview technique as oral history in Black studies', in M.K. Asante and M. Karenga (eds) *Handbook of Black studies*, Thousand Oaks, CA: Sage Publications.

Turney, D. (1996) *The language of anti-racism in social work: Towards a deconstructive reading*, London: University of London.

Tweedie, N. (2006) 'Multi-culturalism may have fractured society, admits Kelly', *The Daily Telegraph*, 24 August (www.telegraph.co.uk/news/main.jhtml;jsessionid=QYGL23TO244M5QFIQMFSFFWAVCBQ0IV0?xml=/news/2006/08/24/nkelly24.xml).

US DHHS (US Department of Health and Human Services) (2001) *Mental health: A report of the Surgeon General (Ch 2)*, Rockville, MD: Author.

Van Soest, D. and Garcia, B. (2003) *Diversity education for social justice*, Alexandria, VA: Council for Social Work Education.

Victor, C. (2005) *The social context of ageing: A textbook of gerontology*, Oxfordshire: Routledge.

Webb, E., Maddocks, A. and Bongilli, J. (2002) 'Effectively protecting black and minority ethnic children from harm: overcoming barriers to the child protection process', *Child Abuse Review*, vol 11, no 6, pp 394-410.

Wells Irme, R. (1984) 'The nature of knowledge in social work', *Social Work*, vol 29, pp 41-5.

West, C. (1994) *Race matters*, New York, NY: Vintage Press.

Westwood, S. (1989) *Sadness in my heart: Racism and mental health*, Leicester: Leicester Black Mental Health Group.

White, J.L. (1984) *The psychology of blacks*, Englewood Cliffs, NJ: Prentice Hall.

Williams, C. (1999) 'Connecting anti-racist and anti-oppressive theory and practice: retrenchment or reappraisal?', *British Journal of Social Work*, vol 29, no 2, pp 211-30.

Williams, C. and Soydan, H. (2005) 'When and how does ethnicity matter? A cross-national study of social work responses to ethnicity in child protection cases', *British Journal of Social Work*, vol 35, no 6, pp 901-20.

Williams, D. and Williams-Morris, R. (2000) 'Racism and mental health: the African American experience', *Ethnicity and Health*, vol 5, no 3/4, pp 243-68.

Williams, E. (1964) *Capitalism and slavery*, London: Andre Deutsch.

Williams, F. (1987) 'Racism and the discipline of social policy', *Critical Social Policy*, vol 20, September, pp 4-59.

Williams, F. (2000) 'Travels with nanny. Destination good enough. A personal/intellectual journey through the welfare state', Inaugural lecture, University of Leeds, 11 May (www.leeds.ac.uk/CAVA).

Williams, F. (2004) 'What matters is who works: why every child matters to New Labour, Commentary on the DfES Green Paper *Every Child Matters*', *Critical Social Policy*, vol 24, no 3, pp 406-27.

Wilson, G. (2000) *Understanding old age: Critical and global perspectives*, Thousand Oaks, CA: Sage Publications.

Wilson, M. (2001) 'Black women and mental health', *Feminist Review*, no 68, Summer, pp 34-51.

Wilson, W.J. (1980) *The declining significance of race: Blacks and changing American institutions* (2nd edn), Chicago, IL: University of Chicago Press.

Worsley, P. (1973) *Problems in modern society*, London: Penguin Books.

Wrench, J. (2005) 'Diversity management can be bad for you', *Race and Class*, vol 46, no 3, pp 73-84.

Young, I.M. (1989) 'Polity and group difference: a critique of the ideal of universal citizenship', *Ethics*, vol 99, no 2, pp 250-74.

Young, I.M. (1990) *Justice and the politics of difference*, Princeton, NJ: Princeton University Press.

Index